## *Examine Life's M...*

*ESP, Witches and UFOs* ... two-volume set of Hans Holzer's best works. In this anthology, best-selling author and psychic investigator Hans Holzer explores true accounts of the strange and unknown: telepathy, psychic and reincarnation dreams, survival after death, psycho-ecstasy, unorthodox healing, Pagans and Witches, and Ufonauts. Included in this volume:

- Mrs. F. dreamed of a group of killers and was particularly frightened by the eyes of the leader. Ten days later, the Sharon Tate murders broke into the headlines. When Mrs. F. saw the photo of Charles Manson, she immediately recognized him as the man from her dream.
- Telepathic messages relayed over two continents thousands of miles apart.
- How you can use four simple steps to achieve psycho-ecstasy: turning a negative situation into something positive and desirable.
- True accounts of miraculous healings achieved through unorthodox methods.
- Eyewitness reports of UFO landings and the interaction between otherworldly beings and humans.
- The reasons why more and more people are turning to Witchcraft and Paganism—not only as a religion, but as a way of life.
- Authentic out-of-the-body experiences in which astral travel and past life regression occurred.

These reports and many more will entertain and enlighten all readers intrigued by the mysteries of the human mind, the universe and beyond!

## About the Author
Hans Holzer's interest in parapsychology started early in life—at age three! As a precocious, inquisitive nine year old in Vienna, Austria, he began writing poems and dramas on the subject of ghosts and performed experiments in "raising the dead."

Holzer went on to earn a Ph.D., and today Dr. Holzer is the author of eighty-nine books mainly dealing with psychic subjects and investigations of the paranormal. He has taught parapsychology for many years at the New York Institute of Technology and lectures extensively. Holzer also writes and produces television and feature films, and is a regular guest on television and radio talk shows.

## To Write to the Author
We cannot guarantee that every letter written to the author can be answered, but all will be forwarded. Both the author and the publisher appreciate hearing from readers, learning of your enjoyment and benefit from this book. Llewellyn also publishes a bi-monthly news magazine with news and reviews of practical esoteric studies and articles helpful to the student, and some readers' questions and comments to the author may be answered through this magazine's columns if permission to do so is included in the original letter. The author sometimes participates in seminars and workshops, and dates and places are announced in *The Llewellyn New Times*. To write to the author, or to ask a question, write to:

**Hans Holzer**
**c/o THE LLEWELLYN NEW TIMES**
P.O. Box 64383-368-X, St. Paul, MN 55164-0383, U.S.A.
Please enclose a self-addressed, stamped envelope for reply, or $1.00 to cover costs.

**FATE Presents**

# ESP, Witches and UFOs

## The Best of Hans Holzer, Book II

Edited by Raymond Buckland

1991
Llewellyn Publications
St. Paul, Minnesota 55164-0383, U.S.A.

*ESP, Witches and UFOs* copyright © 1991 by Hans Holzer. All rights reserved. Printed in the United States of America. No part of this book may be used or reproduced in any manner whatsoever without written permission from Llewellyn Publications except in the case of brief quotations embodied in critical articles and reviews.

Cover art by Martin Cannon

Library of Congress Cataloging-in-Publication Data

Holzer, Hans, date.
    ESP, witches, and UFOs /edited by
Raymond Buckland. — 1st ed.
      p.   cm. — (Fate presents)  (The Best of Hans Holzer ; bk. 2)
    ISBN 0-87542-368-X
    1. Parapsychology. 2. Reincarnation. 3. Medicine, Magic, mystic, and spagiric. 4. Witchcraft. 5. Unidentified flying objects. I. Buckland, Raymond. II. Title. III. Series. IV. Series : Holzer, Hans—Selections. 1990 ; bk. 2.
BF1031.H665   1990                                90-29142
133—dc20                                                  CIP

Llewellyn Publications
A Division of Llewellyn Worldwide, Ltd.
P.O. Box 64383, St. Paul, MN 55164-0383

# About the FATE Presents Series

Since 1948, FATE magazine has brought to readers around the world true, documented reports of the strange and unusual. For over four decades FATE has reported on such subjects as UFOs and space aliens, Bigfoot, the Loch Ness monster, ESP, psychic powers, divination, ghosts and poltergeists, startling new scientific theories and breakthroughs, real magic, near-death and out-of-body experiences, survival after death, Witches and Witchcraft and many other topics that will even astound your imagination.

FATE has revealed the fakers and the frauds and examined the events and people with powers that defy explanation. If you read it in FATE, the information was certified and factual.

One of the things that makes FATE special is the wide variety of authors who write for it. Some of them have numerous books to their credit and are highly respected in their fields of specialty. Others are plain folks—like you and me—whose lives have crossed over into the world of the paranormal.

Now we are publishing a series of books bearing the FATE name. You hold one such book in your hands. The topic of this book may be one of any of the subjects we've described or a variety of them. It may be a collection of authenticated articles by unknown writers or a book by an author of world-renown.

There is one thing of which you can be assured: the occurrences described in this book are absolutely accurate and took place as noted. Now even more people will be able to marvel at, be shocked by and enjoy *true reports of the strange and unknown*.

# Other Books by Hans Holzer

*Ghosts, Hauntings and Possessions: The Best of Hans Holzer, Book I*

# CONTENTS

| | |
|---|---|
| Introduction | ix |
| Telepathy and How It Works | 1 |
| What Exactly Is a Dream? | 27 |
| Prophetic Dreams | 41 |
| Reincarnation Dreams | 63 |
| The Evidence for Survival After Death | 85 |
| How to Overcome Negativity | 111 |
| Medical Men and Unorthodox Healing | 123 |
| Healing and the Occult Sciences | 167 |
| Witchcraft Is Alive and Well | 179 |
| When UFOs Land: Physical Evidence vs. Cultists | 193 |
| Where Do UFOs Come From and Why? | 231 |

# INTRODUCTION

Hans Holzer's prolific writings cover a wide variety of subjects under the metaphysical (or "New Age") umbrella. Dreams and extrasensory perception have always been big interests of his. He has also written a number of books on contemporary Witchcraft and paganism, as well as a book on the ever-fascinating subject of UFOs and visitors from other worlds. In this second volume of *The Best Of Hans Holzer* he examines these things, in his usual thorough way, and explains them for the benefit of newcomer and seasoned student alike.

Many people have preconceived ideas on most of these subjects. Frequently ideas held over a lifetime; ideas oftimes inherited from parents and elders. But today the world is changing rapidly, with new discoveries and tremendous advances, almost on a daily basis. Many of us are having to adjust our thinking; to accept ideas that may have been anathema to us twenty years ago, or less. And this, the dawning of the Age of Aquarius, is a good time to rethink our positions—even to start thinking for ourselves! As Professor Holzer says in the introduction to his book *Possessed,* "Change does of necessity indicate the ending of one period and the beginning of another. Old ideas and new ideas on the same subject cannot possibly coexist. There has to be destruction in order to build up."

So it is with much of what we find in this and the previous volume. New ideas. New evidence to endorse, correct, or supplant the old. This is how we move forward. As it happens, the whole area of parapsychology and psychical research is so relatively new that there is not a true changeover from old to new, simply because there is no "old"! Yet even in the short time that serious investigation has been around there has been a tremendous move forward in the methods of investigation and in the willingness to accept some of the surprising results obtained.

What of the future? As Hans would tell you, we have not yet begun to scratch the surface. There is a whole world of fascinating and intriguing material out there, just waiting to be investigated. Just to take one example—UFOs and extraterrestrial incursions into our world. Where do they come from? Why do they come here? How do we make and keep contact? What can we learn? This is just one subject in this wide and wonderful world. I hope that Hans Holzer's writings will inspire many of his readers to take up the torch and carry light into dark corners; to follow in his footsteps and explore these new, yet old, worlds.

Raymond Buckland

# TELEPATHY AND HOW IT WORKS

## *(ESP and You)*\*

Probably the best known form of ESP, and at the same time the least understood, is telepathy, not "mental telepathy" as some people redundantly call it.

Strictly speaking, the term in Greek merely means "impression across a distance." To the parapsychologist it represents the simplest form of extrasensory perception. Another name given this faculty at times is "thought transference," but I prefer to describe the ability of telepathic communication—whether as sender or as receiver—as knowledge gained without the use of the ordinary five senses.

First of all, let me define "thought" as the image or set of conditions created in the mind of one person, or the observation of existing conditions by a person in which he or she takes note of what is perceived through the ordinary five senses. In my opinion, a thought is also an electric impulse very much like a radio message, sent out by means of

---

\* The parenthetical title appearing after each chapter heading indicates the book from which excerpts were taken.

the brain (as different from the mind, which operates through the brain but is not identical with it). Since it is an electric entity, a thought must naturally have some body or substance, no matter how small, and therefore one should be capable of registering, measuring, or, in some other neutral, non-subjective way, tracing its existence.

What orthodox medicine likes to call "brain waves" have long been measured by the electroencephalograph, an apparatus capable of registering, through electrodes attached to the head, the tiny currents within a patient's brain.

When a person has an "idea," it means that a thought wave has already been created and sent out by the brain. Ordinarily, humans cannot control either direction or intensity of this "broadcast." However, some particularly endowed people can be trained to use thought messages in a way that they will be received by a particular receiver on the other end of the invisible line. We then have a two-way experiment which is capable of being rigidly controlled by the simple method of examining the information received by the receiver. If he or she had no foreknowledge of the contents, or any access to the information contained in it, yet the material checks out as true in specific respects, then we have a clear-cut case of successful "thought transference," or telepathy.

Probably the best known of these experiments in recent years was the exchange of thought messages between Harold Sherman, mentalist and author, and the Arctic explorer, Sir Hubert Wilkins. It all happened in 1937, when Wilkins, an

Australian, led a rescue mission to the North Pole to find some Russian aviators who had crashed on the ice. Long interested in telepathy, Wilkins arranged with Sherman to attempt regular communications across the miles via mental messages.

Sherman would sit at certain intervals, three times a week, in his New York apartment, while Wilkins was out there looking for the lost flyers. Wilkins would send thoughts to Sherman, while keeping a diary, and Sherman did the same in New York.

Each night, the two experimenters sent records of their activities separately to Dr. Gardner Murphy, now president of the American Society for Psychic Research. When the material was compared by Dr. Murphy, it was found that over 70% of the entries were correct, that is, identical.

Occasionally, Sherman managed a kind of "television" telepathy as well as the more ordinary "radio" telepathy. On Armistice Day, 1937, Sherman saw, in his mind's eye, Wilkin's plane forced down in a blizzard and right afterwards he perceived an image of the explorer waltzing at a ball, wearing a full dress suit! This made very little sense to him, consciously, of course.

Ten days later Wilkin's own report arrived. On an emergency flight to Saskatchewan, his plane had been forced down at Regina during a blizzard. There the governor had invited him to attend an Armistice Day Ball! The distance between the two men was roughly 3500 miles, but distance and time barriers do not exist in the realms of extrasensory perception.

Later, Sherman allowed himself to be tested by Hollywood producer Ivan Tors, whose curiosity he had aroused. In the presence of several doctors, Sherman was placed in a small office and the door closed. For half an hour he jotted down random impressions received by him telepathically.

Tors had meanwhile gone on location to work on a motion picture he was producing at the time. Sherman's notes were 80% correct, involving some intricate details of the shooting, the unforeseen problems Tors encountered, and things that had happened to the producer that day.

This, of course, is different from sending clear-cut messages through space. Here we have a telepathic medium, Sherman, picking up random thoughts and situations at a distance, not expressly beamed at him. Still, it worked.

In scientific language, "cross correspondences" are controlled experiments, often long distance, in which a psychic person gets impressions of situations—while a scientific team of observers at the other end also records what it sees or what is happening. There are many well-documented cases of this.

Typical perhaps is an experiment I myself am familiar with, which was undertaken about ten years ago in New York City. At that time, a group assembled on the Lower West Side, watched as a young man named Stanley went into a trance state, in which he was able to project himself to a designated location some distance away. Naturally, he knew nothing about that location beforehand. The other team had arranged a rose in a vase and a book opened at a certain page as markers in the apartment that Stanley was to visit telepathically.

On his "return," Stanley described what he had seen quite accurately. He could not have obtained this knowledge from those around him, since they did not know the details of the other apartment.

The question, however, arises whether Stanley received a picture of the place from the minds of those present in the apartment, which would be telepathy, or whether he himself was able to project his "etheric self," his own person, to the place—that is, leave his body temporarily, observe what he could, and then return. This is called astral projection, and is quite common, both the voluntary and the involuntary kind.

I am convinced that many telepathic experiments involve this kind of projection. "Pure" telepathy, where the receiver does not go any place, but merely concentrates on getting messages or impressions, is much more common in spontaneous cases, that is, cases not anticipated or experimentally induced.

The dividing line between telepathy, clairvoyance or precognition (foretelling of future events), and astral projection (apparent travel of the "inner body" while asleep or entranced) is very uncertain. It is so badly drawn, in fact, that I have long suspected that it does not exist at all.

True, we must label experiences *somehow* if we are to proceed cautiously and scientifically to explore and explain them, but I rather think that all psychic experiences are of one kind. Just as there are short and tall people and people who speak different languages or have different backgrounds, yet are all human—so I feel that these various *aspects* of sixth-sense experiences are merely varying forms of the same force, differing in specific circumstances but not in origin.

Simple thought transference, telepathy without the possibility of other explanations, works best when there is a compelling reason for it. If there is an emotional urgency in transmitting a message, or if normal means of communication are out, then it works even better.

Several years ago I was attending a play rehearsal in New York when I suddenly remembered that I had made an appointment with the lyricist John Latouche for 5 P.M. that day. The set being closed and no telephone nearby, I became increasingly unhappy at the thought of having to disappoint my distinguished friend. My preoccupation was noticed by one of the singers present, a psychically gifted young lady named Future Fulton. I explained my inability to let Latouche know I would be late, and how I wished I could send him a message to that effect.

"Is that all? she asked, closed her eyes for a moment, breathed deeply, and then, reopening her eyes added, "The message has been delivered."

I laughed a little uncertainly, and went on with the work at hand. When I returned home around six, I quickly telephoned Latouche and started to apologize for not having called him earlier.

"What are you talking about?" Latouche interjected. "You most certainly did. Why, my answering service tells me *someone* called at five to say you'd be delayed."

Telepathy works best between people who know each other, and even better between people who are emotionally close to each other. This is no more astounding than the fact that an electric plug fits best into a socket especially made for it, or that a stage director likes to work with actors he or she knows already because they can communicate better with each other. Two radios tuned in on one another naturally yield better results than a random beam looking for a receiver and losing its energy while searching a very large field.

I have already stated that all extrasensory experiences are emotionally tinged in that they involve the whole personality. The emotions need not be love or hatred. Creative excitement is an equally strong emotional force. Many ideas seem to have been "in the air" only to be picked up simultaneously, and quite independently from each other, by a number of people. The same inventions are made in widely separated areas, and music is written by people who don't know of each other, and yet duplicate each other's work. Some philosophers want us to believe that there is a "World Mind" whence all knowledge comes—a sort of super public domain ready to be tapped by anyone with the right tools.

But it may be just one mind, giving out strong thought waves, and another at a distance, receiving them without realizing that the new idea he or she has suddenly hit upon really originated in someone else's mind. Innocent plagiarism, perhaps, and the world is full of this kind of "coincidence."

Particularly strange things happen to identical twins. Apparently the ties of their physical birth extend into the psychic realm as well. They will feel pain at the same time, even though separated by distance, and can frequently read each other's thoughts. The Young twins of Jackson, Mississippi were recently tested by Mississippi State University psychologist Ophelia Rivers, who found them exceptional in their ability to convey thoughts to each other.

Practically speaking, telepathy is a faculty everybody may have deeply imbedded within his or her personality, but only those capable of being "good senders" or "good receivers" will make practical use of this most valuable talent.

Here then are some hints how you can achieve this; that is, if you are honestly interested and not "scared" of something that is perfectly natural. Fear inhibits all forms of extrasensory perception.

Learn to remove all prejudices on the subject, have no preconceived notions whether it will "work for you" or not. Your doubting will surely make you fail. Cautious optimism—that it may well work—is the best attitude to take. Above all, relax and don't strain or force. Tension is your enemy. A carefree, unperturbed, and above all, unhurried attitude is helpful. Don't restrict your experiments to rigid schedules. Don't insist it must work by next week or else. Let go of yourself, allow it to happen and sooner or later it may.

Visualize the person to whom you wish to transmit your thoughts, if you are to be the sender. Check with the other person at intervals to see if you have indeed succeeded, but do not alert the other person. This is not a controlled scientific experiment, and if the other person is aware of your efforts he or she may also tense up, making it twice as hard to get through. If the receiver does not know when and what will be transmitted telepathically, you have an open door on the other end.

The best telepathy occurs when the thought being sent out is conceived spontaneously, without trying. For instance, you have a sudden thought how nice it is to see your mother again. Your mother lives five hundred miles away. Just at that instant, she also suddenly thinks of you and how nice it would be to see you. Coincidence? Not when it happens in thousands of cases, many of them easy to verify. There is something about thoughts that is very much like radio waves. They travel, once emitted, in every direction until their energies have thinned out to such an extent that they are no longer capable of being received.

Since thought waves, very much like other radiation, give off tiny particles of themselves as they travel along, they gradually become weaker. However, this loss of energy potential is so small that, for all practical purposes, thought waves can travel great distances without apparent loss of clarity. Thus we have a total disregard for the usual laws of space and time, inasmuch as thought waves do not respect solid objects and other hindrances either. They pierce walls and, in some as yet not fully understood way, are caught or attracted by "tuned in" receivers. There may be more than one receiver. There may be none. Once the thought waves have been created by the sender and are on their way, he or she has no further contact with them.

We do know that thought waves originate in the mind, which uses the brain as its "switchboard." The electricity required to make the process possible is derived from the network of nerve fibers within the human body, which has sufficient voltage for this. In this respect much more research will have to be done to explore the mechanics of transmission, but I daresay it is no different in concept from radio transmission, only on an infinitely finer and more sensitive scale.

Although thoughts originate in the mind and are sent out via the brain, they are received on the other end through the unconscious part of the mind. With trained experimenters, the conscious part of the mind can also be used on occasion to serve as a receiver, but the vast majority of telepathic cases involve spontaneous reception which employs the unconscious (or, if you prefer, subconscious) part of the mind as its gateway.

This eliminates the inhibiting factors of rationalization and rejection, which might otherwise come into play and destroy the message before it is properly evaluated. Since only few people understand the workings of telepathy, the majority of those having such experiences will explain the thought that arises in them, possibly spurring them into action of one kind or another, as a "hunch," or a sudden inspiration.

The shadings of telepathic communication are many and they run the gamut from vague feelings about distant people or events to clear-cut, sharp, and definite messages instantly capable of verification. It depends on both sender and receiver, their individual abilities to free themselves from inhibiting factors, their surroundings, their prejudices, their fears, and the nature or urgency of the message itself.

The stronger the need, and the greater the emergency, the more likely will there be a strong reception. Trifling bits of information are less likely to create such remarkable impressions on the other end of the line. There are cases where the message is nothing more exciting than a friendly hello from a distance. Telepathy has no hard and fast rules. But it works.

What can it do for you?

Lots of things. If you are "aware"—that is, willing to accept messages of this kind—you may well be warned in times of danger by someone at a distance who wishes you well. Conversely, you may do this for someone yourself. It is a distinct thrill when two people who are close, such as husband and wife or good friends, manage to communicate without words—spoken words, that is. Not that it saves wear and tear on their speech mechanisms, but the spark of instant thought flying from mind to mind makes such relationships stronger, and when creative work is involved this can be a blessing. Two partners working together, or two artists or writers—their separate thought processes can be fused into one creative effort!

On a business level, for the salesperson or executive to catch a fleeting thought from the mind of the individual opposite him or her can be very useful. This is not so much mind reading as merely being tuned in on what the other person wishes to put across. Just think how surprised your new boss would be if you say the very things he or she has on his or her mind. On the other hand, if the person you are dealing with is likely to be unreliable, catching a thought wave might very well warn you to be careful.

I do not pretend that everybody can use telepathy in the same way. But *potentially*, at least, it is a lost faculty that can be restored to humans by their assuming the proper attitude, and then allowing actual usage of this faculty to improve it. The more you relax-and-project (instead of concentrate-and-worry), the more chance you will have of coming across from mind to mind.

## The Trinity of Prophecy: Clairvoyance, Clairaudience, Clairsentience

Next to telepathic communication between living persons, incidents of foretelling the future are the most common ESP experiences. In the days of the Bible these were referred to as prophecies, and on their least desirable level they are called fortunetelling—though, heaven knows, the fortune made is mainly that of the fortuneteller. Again, the basic characteristic of the phenomena is a seeming disregard for the conventional boundaries of time and space. Distance in either time or geographical location has no effect on the results of this faculty.

I am convinced that it is one faculty with three different forms of expression. It depends merely on the particular "phase" of the psychic person—that is, the area in which the psychic talent manifests itself. Just as some musicians are good on the piano while others are better with a violin and still others are singers, so we have people who foresee things, others who hear things before they happen, and still others, though least in number, who can get olfactory impressions—peculiar smells associated with events—seemingly ahead of actual occurrence.

Clairvoyants are by far the most numerous. Their visions can be subjective (in the mind's eye) or objective (before them). Clairaudience means the hearing of voices or messages in one's inner ear without seeing the person who speaks. Although clairsentience can also be useful at times, most of the scientifically reliable data can be religious in one's heart and still demand something more. The nature of the deity is a philosophical question but it can and must also be a scientific one if a truly valid religion is ever to be found for *all* of humankind. Probably the closest to an acceptable truth are those who argue that God is within us all and we are all part of God, and that the universe and its clearly established laws are the guiding principles governing our bouts with events in space and time. But it still leaves the question open, who set all this up, who started it, what started it, and when?

I wish I knew the answer, but I don't. Yet.

### Astral Projection, or Going Places Without Body

Out-of-the-body experiences are far more common than one would think, but the majority of people to whom they happen either prefer to keep still about them out of fear of ridicule or worse, or they simply don't understand them and put it all down to a bad dream.

It was only a few years ago that Sylvan Muldoon and Dr. Carrington explained these phenomena logically in a book considered a classic on astral flight. Muldoon was the flyer and Carrington the investigator. I have touched briefly before on experimental astral projection, undertaken under controlled conditions and with research teams supervising all phases.

That this type of experiment is not without danger is known, and Madame Blavatzky's warning not to try it in her works dealing with theosophy is not to be taken lightly. Mental derangement can result when shock prevents the proper return and "resettlement" of the non-physical part of a human being into his or her physical abode, the body. Everything has to sink back into place or damage results.

Let me hasten to explain how astral projection works. The typical case consists of a person suddenly having a sensation of rising slowly from his or her own body, usually late at night or early in the morning when the consciousness level is low. However, many cases involve people fully awake, for astral flight is by no means reserved to the dream state. These people at first feel frightened and confused, especially when they see their own body sleeping below them.

Sometimes they find themselves standing in a corner of their room looking back at "themselves" and wondering whether they are dead; sometimes they are drawn out into the countryside at great speed and find themselves actually traveling to distant places. During these rapid transits, they are fully aware of themselves as people, but the world around them, invariably, is described in terms of awe—everything seems more acute— more sharply defined—than in the normal state.

Some astral travelers speak of a bluish-white light that illuminates everything, and they have no difficulty seeing through or passing through walls and walking about other people's houses. Mainly, they will visit people or places that they have consciously or unconsciously desired to see for some time, but on occasion they find themselves in places they are not familiar with at all.

Once present in a location other than their beds, these astral travelers are fully able to function as observers in every respect. In fact, frequently, they are keener and remember in greater detail what they witness than they would have had they entered through the door encased in their physical bodies!

This shows that our physical bodies actually encumber our senses and that our true personalities can do better when we use our etheric counterparts, our so-called inner eyes, inner ears, etc. This applies, it appears, both in the temporary absence from the physical body called astral projection, and in the permanent exile called death.

The only difference is the presence or absence of a thin, shiny connecting link usually called the silver cord, which connects the astral personality to its physical body very much like a breathing apparatus links the deep-sea diver with the control station aboard ship on the surface of the sea.

Once it is cut, the person cannot be pulled back to the body and is what we call "dead." That this can happen accidentally on these astral excursions is true, but it is extremely rare and would imply great lack of caution on the part of the traveler, or, of course, interference with the body left behind "sleeping" by someone unaware of the true situation.

Indeed, that is the principal danger of astral projection, and it is recommended that a person who finds that he or she has this psychic gift should always lock the doors at night and leave explicit instructions not to try to "arouse" him or her!

I realize how difficult this might be in our skeptical days, but there is no other alternative to protect oneself, for you cannot suppress involuntary astral projection anymore than you can stop the mind from thinking.

From a scientific control point of view, astral

projection is mainly a subjective experience and only the large volume of parallel testimony can give clues to its operational setup. However, there are a number of verified cases on record where the astral traveler was actually seen, heard, or felt by those at the other end of the trip, thus corroborating a subjective experience by objective observation.

That time is truly a convention and not an independent dimension at all can be seen from the fact that differences in regional observation times in such cases are always adjusted to coincide with the proper local time: if any astrally projected person is seen in his or her etheric or non-physical state at 3 P.M. in Los Angeles, and the traveler him or herself recalls his or her experience in New York to have taken place at exactly 6 P.M., we know that the time differential between California and the Eastern Seaboard is three hours and thus practically no measurable time seems to have elapsed between the commencement and the completion of the astral trip.

That a tiny amount of what we call time does elapse I am sure, for the speed of astral travel cannot be greater than the speed of thought, the ultimate according to Einstein (and not the speed of light, as formerly thought). Even thought takes time to travel, although it can cover huge distances in fractions of a second. But thought—and astral projection—are electric impulses and cannot travel entirely without some loss of the time element, no matter how tiny this loss is. Someday, when we have built apparatus to measure these occurrences, it will no doubt be found that a tiny delay factor does exist between the two ends of the astral road.

The duration of astral flight varies according to the relaxed state of the projected person. A very nervous, fearful individual need only panic and desire to be in his or her own bed—and pronto, is pulled back, nay, snapped back, into his or her body with rubberband-like impact and some subsequent unpleasantness.

The sensation, according to many who have experienced this, is like falling from great heights or spinning down in a mad spiral and waking up suddenly in one's bed as if from a bad dream, which in a way it is.

I am convinced that the falling sensation is not due to any actual physical fall at all, but merely represents the sudden deceleration of the vibratory speed of the person. Astral travel, like all psychic life, is at a much higher rate of speed than is physical life. Thus when the personality is suddenly yanked off the road, so to speak, and forcibly slowed down very quickly, a shock-like condition results. The denser atmosphere in which our physical bodies move requires a slower rate of pulsation. Normally, in astral projection, the person returns gradually to his or her body and the process is orderly and gradual, so no ill effects result. But when the return is too sudden there is no time for this, and the screeching coming to a stop of the bodily vehicle is the result.

Psychiatrists have tried to explain the very common sensation of falling from great heights in one's dream as an expression of fear. The trouble with this explanation is that the experience is so common that it could not possibly cover all the people who have had it; many of them do not have unexpressed fears or fear complexes. Also, some astral travelers have had this while partially or fully awake.

I think it is a purely mechanical symptom in which the etheric body is forced to snap back into the physical body at too fast a rate of speed. No permanent injury results, to be sure. The moments of confusion that follow are no worse than the mental fogginess that one often feels on awaking after a vivid dream, without astral projection involved. However, many travelers find themselves strangely tired, as if physical energies had been used up, which indeed they have!

One such person, perhaps a typical case, is Dorothy W., who is a young grandmother in her fifties. She is a mentally and physically alert and well-adjusted person who works as an executive secretary for a large community center. Dorothy has had many psychic experiences involving premonitions of impending death, and has been visited by the shades of the departed on several occasions. She takes these things in stride and is neither alarmed nor unduly concerned over them.

Frequently, she finds that her dream-state is a very tiring one. She visits places known and unknown, and meets people she knows and others she does not know. Those that she recognizes she knows are dead in the conventional sense. She cannot prevent these nocturnal excursions and she has learned to live with them. What is annoying to her, however, is that on awakening she finds her feet physically tired, as if she has been walking for miles and miles!

A typical case where corroboration is available from the other end of the trip is in the files of the American Society for Psychic Research, which made it available to *True* magazine for a report on extrasensory perception. The case involves a young lady whom the society calls Betsy, who traveled astrally to her mother's house over a thousand miles away. In what the report described as a kind of vivid dream state, Betsy saw herself projected to her mother's house.

> After I entered, I leaned against the dish cupboard with folded arms, a pose I often assume. I looked at my mother, who was bending over something white and doing something with her hands. She did not appear to see me at first, but she finally looked up. I had a sort of pleased feeling, and then after standing a second more, I turned and walked about four steps.

At this point, Betsy awoke. The clock at her bedside showed the time as 2:10 A.M. The impression that she had actually just seen (and been seen by) her mother a thousand miles away was so overwhelming that the next morning Betsy wrote her mother asking whether she had experienced anything unusual that night.

The mother's reply in part follows: "Why

don't you stay home and not go gallivanting so far from home when you sleep? Did you know you were here for a few seconds?" The mother said it was 1:10 A.M. on the night in question. Her letter continued: "It would have been 10 after 2 your time. I was pressing a blouse here in the kitchen—I couldn't sleep either. I looked up and there you were by the cupboard, just standing smiling at me. I started to speak and saw you were gone." The girl, according to the mother (who saw her only from the waist up), wore the light blouse of her dream.

Finally, there is a kind of semi-voluntary astral projection, where a person wills him or herself to visit a distant place itself or its appearance. When such a visit yields verified details, no matter how seemingly small or insignificant, we can judge the verity of the experiment so much more accurately.

Some researchers refer to this particular phase also as "traveling clairvoyance." Others maintain that really only a part of the personality doing the projecting is visiting distant places and that the essential portion of oneself does not move. To me, this is harder to believe than the more natural explanation of duality—the physical body stays behind and the etheric body travels. Not a part of the etheric body, but all of it.

What about thought projections then? There are known cases where an apparition of a *living* person has suddenly and momentarily appeared to others in the flesh great distances away. Usually, there are emotional situations involved in this type of phenomenon. Either the apparition of the living is to warn of impending disaster or danger, or the sender him or herself is in trouble and seeks help. But the projection is sudden and momentary in all cases and does not compare to the lingering qualities of a true ghost or an apparition of a person who is deceased.

I am inclined to think that these thought projections in which a living person appears to another living person are extremely fast astral projections, so fast, in fact, that the etheric body is back home again before the traveler realizes it, and that, therefore, there is no need to be in a prone position in bed—a sudden sense of absence, of being not all there, at the most.

I can recall Eileen Garrett telling me of an incident concerning the late John Latouche, who was a pretty good medium himself. Over lunch one day in New York, Eileen suddenly noticed John's blank stare: for a minute or two John had been astrally traveling—a total displacement in time and space. It was all over so quickly that neither spoke about it.

While doing research for my book *Ghost Hunter*, I met a young Japanese-American woman by the name of Mia Yamaoka who had had psychic experiences on several occasions. One particular phase of her ESP talents that interested me was her apparent ability to send herself off by astral projection—not in controlled experiments with teams of researchers on both ends, to be sure, but propelled by an emotional, personal need to make contact with relatives with whom she had lost touch.

She had read an instruction book on self-hypnosis and followed its instructions on how to relax properly.

I lay on the bed and concentrated on a small object near the ceiling. I followed the instructions in the hypnosis book, telling myself to relax, and that I was sleepy, and breathed deeply and began to count. After doing this a few times, I felt my body rising to the ceiling, and I gave myself instructions to visit a sister who was in a hospital in Los Angeles. (I was in New York.) As I rose to the ceiling, I was aware that my other body was still lying in bed (or I had such an impression). Suddenly I seemed to zoom out of the room through the window side of the wall, but not necessarily out of the window. I seemed to be flying through the air. I passed buildings and even passed through them, seeing people asleep in their beds, but passing through walls and rooms. I also recall that the sky was dark blue when I was flying through the air where there were no buildings. Then I saw the ocean waves lapping on some large rocks and the thought came to me that I must be on the West Coast. Suddenly, I landed on a large green lawn. In the distance was a building such as a hospital. My sister appeared, and since we had not seen each other for about 19 or 20 years, we cried and embraced each other.

I studied her face and noted that she had aged from the time I had last seen her. I was conscious of the thought that I should remember something to verify this visit, and I studied her dress carefully. She had on a white dress with black rickrack trimming.

A week or so after the first experience, I decided to try again and visit one of my other sisters. This sister, S.L., was also in Los Angeles. My experience was the same. I flew just as I had before. I seemed to reach Los Angeles in "a twinkling of an eye." I saw the water lapping on the rocky shore, then I found myself on a street. There was a small house recessed back from the street. There were some trees in front of the house, but the house could be seen, and I noticed a small porch. I had not heard from my sister, S.L., for about two years, and the last time I had heard from her, she had been living in an apartment house. Therefore, the thought came to me that this could not be the place where S.L. lived. However, I called her name a few times timidly, and no one appeared. I decided to verify this visit, if possible, but found it hard to write in a letter. Especially since I had not heard from S.L. for a while, and did not know her address.

Finally, I wrote a letter, addressed to S.L.'s last known address, asking the letter to be forwarded, which it was in a rather round-about way. My sister, S.L., then began to correspond again.

About a month ago, I had occasion to visit Los Angeles and saw my sister. I explained my experience to her, and described the house. She said I described exactly the house that she had lived in at that time. She verified that it was a small house with a small porch (the porch was not the entire length of the house), it was in the back of a lot, and there were trees in front of it.

# WHAT EXACTLY IS A DREAM?

## *(The Psychic Side of Dreams)*

Even some pretty well educated people frequently do not know the difference between sleep and dream, that is, they are not cognizant of the fact that certain processes occur during the sleep stage while others occur only while an individual is dreaming. This is of course understandable since sleep and dream come together, as it were, occupying the same period in the time continuum. But they are not identical—to sleep does not necessarily mean to dream, and there are states of dreaming that are not truly part of the sleep state, in which a person can come pretty close to being awake though not fully conscious. The majority of dreams, however, certainly occur while a person is asleep. In fact, I would prefer to say one is either asleep or awake, and one can be asleep and "adream" at the same time. Of course, not remembering a dream does not mean that a dream, or dreams, has not occurred. Individual observation of the dream state, while it is the primary source of content, is nevertheless not reliable in an objective way. The dream memory fades quickly upon awakening and the sleeper may simply not remember. Although some materialistically inclined people tend to dismiss dreaming as the equivalent of fantasizing, this was not always so. Prior to nineteenth-century materialism, dreaming was considered serious business. William Shakespeare frequently refers to the dream state as a state of great significance. "To sleep: perchance to dream ..." (*Hamlet*) and "We are such stuff as dreams are made on" (*The Tempest*) are two of the better-known quotations which indicate how important Shakespeare and his contemporaries found dream material to be to the creative and intellectual processes in humans.

What exactly happens to body, mind and spirit when we are asleep? How do dreams come into being? According to Sandra Shulman, English writer on comparative religion, oneirology, or the study and interpretation of dreams, was originally associated and inseparably tied in with the mystic roots of civilization, religion and magic, to which medicine was also closely tied. She says, "Dreams might have remained in the nebulous atmosphere of poetry, superstition, and fairground quackery, but at the end of the last century a Viennese doctor, Sigmund Freud, saw them as the keys with which to unlock the doors of man's unconscious."

But what hath Freud wrought? Nothing less than the total rejection by establishment scientists and those following them of the ancient wisdoms contained in pre-Freud dream interpretation, nothing less than the rejection of the they are due to our inability to solve our problems in the waking state.

A somewhat different approach is taken by Erich Fromm, internationally recognized authority on psychology and author of a number of works, among which I consider *The Art of Loving* perhaps the most monumental contribution to human understanding. In a recent book entitled *The Forgotten Language,* Dr. Fromm says that it is more important to deal with the understanding of dreams than with their interpretation. He considers dreams to contain symbolic language, which he calls a language in its own right, "in fact the only universal language the human race ever developed," and he sees the problem of dealing with dream material one of understanding this symbolism rather than looking for some artifically created code. "I believe that each understanding is important for every person who wants to be in touch with himself, and not only for the psychotherapist who wants to cure mental disturbances." Dr. Fromm goes on to quote from the Talmud, the sacred Hebrew book of learning, "a dream which is not understood is like a letter which is not opened."

Where Dr. Hall flatly refuses to recognize dream material as anything but hallucinatory, Dr. Fromm says, "The dream is present, real experience, so much so, indeed, that it suggests two questions: what is reality? how do we know that what we dream is unreal and what we experience in our waking life is real?" The Italian playwright Luigi Pirandello has fashioned several dramas on this theme. Where Freud and his disciples tended to look to dreams as expressions of unresolved libido conflicts, Fromm sees in them symbolic material, which, incidentally, is identical no matter what background the dreamer may have, no matter what kind of people are concerned. A truly universal form of expression, Dr. Fromm feels that the symbolic language of dreams is "a language in which inner experiences, feelings and thoughts are expressed as if they were sensory experiences, events in the outer world. It is a language which has a different logic from the conventional one we speak in the daytime, a logic in which not time and space are the ruling categories, but intensity and association."

But dreams are all of those things, and more. To begin with, the dream state covers such a large segment of human experience that it nearly rivals the waking state, although it may occupy only a fraction of the conventional time spent by humans while awake. I consider the dream state a state of *heightened receptiveness*, necessary to convey to humans certain information which they would normally not accept because of the nature of their psyche. In order to perform effectively in the waking state, the unconscious part of the mind is generally shut off or largely subdued. Were it not so, humans would not be able to function as efficiently as they frequently do. On the other hand, concentrating one's energies on purely mechanistic actions results in the suppression and shutting out of the more gentle vibrations of a creative-perceptive nature. Thus it is necessary to have two sets of circumstances if humans are to function properly on *all* levels.

We already know what happens to the human body when we are asleep; the unconscious part of the mind is allowed free range of expression, while the physical body continues to function on a reduced scale, maintaining vital functions by an ingenious system, allowing just enough activity to maintain life, but not enough to intrude into the sleep state. At least, not in a fully balanced, healthy individual. The two other components of human personality, mind and spirit, or psyche, are, however, not necessarily dormant. Freed from the necessity of operating the body vehicle, they can turn their energies toward goals which they are incapable of pursuing when they must look after the body. As far as mind is concerned, as the "guardian of the vehicle," the natural task seems to be the filtering of information from outside, allowing it to come through and reach the unconscious level of mind in order to be understood by the dreamer. A degree of filtering is involved in order to make the material acceptable to the individual. On the other hand, the psyche, or spirit, is now free to send symbolic material upward toward the conscious level so it can be understood when the dreamer awakes.

We thus have a two-way traffic, external material being received and sorted out, and internal material being sent out to the dreamer's conscious, in order to call his or her attention to certain conditions of which he or she is not normally aware. Both processes use imagery in order to express themselves, supplemented by seemingly auditory material, that is to say, the dreamer not only sees scenes but also hears sounds, or feels that he or she does. Since no one else outside the dreamer either sees the same scenes or hears the same sound, they are evidently produced internally, stimulating the respective brain centers directly without the need to go through auditory or visual organs of the body. In a way, this is similar to transferring recordings from one machine to another without the use of an external microphone. The transfer is much the better since unwanted external noises are thus totally eliminated. The dream circuit is also direct and therefore more powerful than if the material were to go through external picture or sound sources.

I have divided the dream material into four major categories: dreams due to physical problems resulting in nightmares or distorted imagery, dreams due to suppressed material and useful for psychoanalytical processes, dreams of a psychic nature, and, finally, out-of-the-body experiences also referred to as astral projection.

As far as physically induced dreams are concerned, there is little quarrel among psychiatrists as to their reality and frequent occurrence. When the body mechanism is loaded down with poisonous substances, through overeating, or other malfunctions of the system, these processes can indeed "press upon" the respective nerve center and cause nightmares or other forms of biochemically induced traumas, albeit of short duration, ending with the restoration of balance in the physical system or the awakening of the dreamer. Even ordinary states of discomfort, such as the need to void, can cause this kind of dream. Only Gypsy dream books would attach importance to expressions of this kind. But it is interesting to note that Dr. Hall sees a connection between such physical dreams and possible paranormal material. In discussing the ancient belief that dreams are produced "by the distemper of the inward parts," he speaks of dreams indicating future illnesses as *prodromic* dreams. The word comes from the Greek for "forerunner" and is interpreted by Dr. Hall as "a premonitory sign of disease." In this ancient belief, dreams of being suffocated or crushed, or of flying, were supposed to indicate the beginnings of a lung disease. Dr. Hall puts emphasis on environmental factors affecting the sleeper as being responsible for certain types of physical dreams, such as a room which is too cold or too warm, or which does not contain enough air, and so on.

It is important to realize that dreams caused by physical pressures do in no way relieve these pressures, nor do they in fact contribute anything to the sleeper's well-being except perhaps by notifying him or her of the existence of some disturbance in the body or environment. This is not surprising since I consider them due to a purely mechanical chain of reactions in the biochemical system of the body, not under the sleeper's control at all, or due to any kind of external forces. The physical system is out of balance due to one or the other cause, and the apparatus reacts in order to call attention to its plight. The moment the system is in balance again, the need for this action no longer exists and the physically induced dreams cease.

Dreams of the second category, due to suppressed material, are the grist for the mills of professional psychoanalysts. If the analyst follows the Freudian line of thinking, he or she will see suppressed libido and sexual symbols in every dream, and will explain the dreams on the basis of sexual maladjustments, needs and symbolisms. If the analyst is a Jungian he or she may do so in a number of cases which are sexual in content, but may explain other dreams as wish-fulfillment dreams or symbolic expressions along the lines of Dr. Erich Fromm. There is no gainsaying that dream material is a valuable tool for psychoanalytical interpretation, that psychoanalysis itself is very useful in many cases. But it is most useful when we are dealing with psychoneurotic individuals, because a psychoneurotic can at times be cured through discussions of his or her suppressed problem. Not so with the psychotic individual, who is much less accessible to discussions of this kind. In that case the dream material becomes merely an informative tool to the doctor, but the two-way dialogue is either non-existent or very much restricted and practical results are therefore harder to obtain.

It is not the purpose of the present book to go into the question of psychoanalytical dream interpretation, except to say that a certain percentage of all dreams do belong in the category of such material, while an equally large and impressive number of dreams do not. Unfortunately, very few trained psychoanalysts understand the difference between symbolic dream material and true psychic dreams. They deal with psychic material as if it were simply symbolic material and as a result distort the interpretation. This is of course due to the fact that the majority of clinical analysts and psychiatrists do not as yet recognize parapsychology as a sister science, or if they do, are not properly trained to apply its principles to their own work. Individual psychiatrists and analysts who do know parapsychological methods are far in between, and the need for more massive training of up-and-coming specialists in this field seems very great. I recall going through psychoanalysis myself in the late 1940s at a time when I was under great external pressure, and thought that analysis would help me understand myself better. My therapist was Dr. E., who had been an assistant to the great Carl Jung. We spent a great deal of time looking over my dream material, and the doctor's method consisted in my first interpreting my own dreams, after which he would interpret them as he saw the material. There were a number of psychic dreams in the lot, and invariably, we came to different conclusions as to their meanings and derivations. After six or seven months I discontinued the sessions, and did not meet Dr. E. until many years later, when Eileen Garrett sponsored a psychotherapy forum in New York City. "I am happy to see you here," Dr. E. said when he recognized me. I shook my head and replied, "No,

Doctor, I am happy to see *you* here." Indeed, Dr. E. had become interested in the work of psychotherapy as practiced by leading parapsychologists of our day.

Before we turn our attention to the remaining two categories of dreams, that is, psychic dreams and out-of-the-body experiences, it is well to state what the differences are between these and conventional dreams. Dreams due to physical discomfort or environmental pressures and dreams of a psychoanalytical connotation are not nearly as vivid as psychic dreams or out-of-the-body experiences. The first two categories of dreams are more easily forgotten upon awakening unless they are immediately written down. Not so with psychic dreams or out-of-the-body experiences; one is rarely able to shake them, even if one does not write them down immediately. Some psychic dreams are so strong that they awaken the dreamer, and in most cases I am familiar with the dream remains clearly etched into the memory for long periods after the dream itself has occurred. Also, with dreams of categories one and two, so-called impossibilities occur with great frequency. Perhaps Dr. Hall's statement that dreams are hallucinatory and not real is understandable in the light of the nature of such dreams. Clearly, dreams in which impossible events take place, mostly out of ordinary time and space sequence, must be hallucinations; but psychic dreams and out-of-the-body experiences are nearly always completely logical sequences of events, frequently entirely possible in terms of ordinary logic, and are received by the dreamer with a sharpness and clarity the first two types of dreams are not.

Although all four categories share a common denominator, that is, the dream state, the first two categories are jumbled, sometimes very confusing bits and pieces of information, while the latter two categories are nearly always complete messages or events, devoid of the fantasy trips and sleight of hand so common with the first two categories of dreams. Of course, there are cases where the categories of dreams get intermingled, and purely symbolic material may become superimposed on true psychic material. This happens where a dreamer is not fully relaxed, or is not a very good recipient of external material. But a skilled parapsychologist can differentiate between the portion of the material properly belonging to category one or two and that representing authentic psychic material.

# PROPHETIC DREAMS

## *(The Psychic Side of Dreams)*

By prophetic dreams I mean all those dreams in which some element, some information is received pertaining to the future, as we know it. In essence something that could not occur by orthodox standards, but which nevertheless does. Prophetic dreams may range all the way from giant prophecies involving entire peoples or the world, to minor concerns of individuals pertaining to their own future or that of friends and relatives. What all prophetic dreams have in common is the element of future events that have not yet transpired, that have not yet begun to shape up in any form whatever, and which therefore could not be foretold by the use of the ordinary five senses.

A frequently heard criticism of prophetic material alludes to the probability factor, or informed guessing on the part of the psychically gifted person. Such arguments are easily disposed of. To begin with, no serious researcher in parapsychology takes a dream at face value unless it contains specific and detailed material of a nature that makes it capable of being verified later on. For example, a psychic announcing that a certain well-known statesman will be deposed or that some great luminary of the screen will remarry or that an aged politician will pass away is of no evidential value, because all of these situations have a high degree of likelihood. If they come to pass it does not disprove the psychic's ability, but it leaves a great margin of doubt whether the psychic was in fact drawing upon his or her inner resources or simply using his or her external reasoning faculties coupled with shrewd phrasing to make these "astonishing" predictions.

In some of my earlier works I made a distinction between prophecy and predictions in that I described prophecy as pertaining to major issues, worldwide situations and prominent individuals, whereas predictions might apply to anyone. A better term for foretelling future events is precognition, implying foreknowledge, whereas predicting means foretelling. Oftentimes the prophecy is visual or perhaps only intuitive and actual words are not used. The common denominator of this material is the future element, something that has not yet come to pass. It is essentially of little significance whether the information comes to the dreamer through visual stimulation, through verbal expressions, through intuitive feelings or through some other form of communication. The essence of it is that the message be clear, precise and sufficiently detailed to warrant the term of prophecy. Prophetic dreams, then, are dreams in which some event or situation pertaining to someone's future is contained and remembered upon awakening. Prophetic material can be obtained in the waking state, too, of course. I have already mentioned that a great percentage of psychic material in general comes unsought to individuals in the dream state because it allows for a deeper and easier penetration of the conscious mind shield. Due to upbringing or our modern approach to phenomena of this kind, most people apply logical values to psychic material coming to them, and in the dream state logic is absent. From the point of view of external individuals wishing to convey messages to human beings, it is easier to get through to them while they are asleep and ready for dreams, than while they are busily engaged in their daily activities. In the dream state, they have a human's full attention, even though he or she must wake up and remember in the end.

It is interesting that some individuals go through psychically active periods while at other times they are unable to have any ESP experiences or else sleep many nights without recalling any unusual dreams. Undoubtedly, the ability to have psychic dreams is connected with the receptiveness of the individual, which in turn has a relationship to physical states, mental conditions and environment, if only concerning the "instrument" through which the material is received. Mrs. S. J. G. of Long Island, New York, explained, "I find that I go into psychic periods when almost every dream will be prophetic or I become more sensitive or even telepathic. I have also learned that if a dream of mine is prophetic, that the time limit in which it will come true is from within a few hours to around six years from the time of the dream."

Frequently psychic people like to have company: when a prophetic dream is particularly upsetting, they take some consolation from similar dreams by other psychics, especially by well-known ones. Mrs. G. dreamt that the United States would be attacked by an atomic power, and she was shown the areas in which the attack would occur. The dream occurred to her in 1970, and she took great comfort from a similar prediction published by me in 1968, according to which we would be attacked on December 29, 1970. Happily, this prediction turned out to be out of date, if not false. Equally unreliable is the date of a similar prediction made by celebrated Chicago psychic Irene Hughes, who foresaw such an event around 1973. But mediums frequently foresee events without getting exact dates, or they may be off by considerable spans of time. It would be foolish to dismiss some prophetic dreams just because the date for the predicted event has come and gone without the event transpiring. Mrs. G. says, "Although I have many prophetic dreams I can never be sure when one is a prophetic dream and when not. There is one clue: my prophetic dreams are very definite in their message. There is no symbolism, such as with most dreams. I see the events and actions as they will happen. The message is clear and not surrounded with symbols."

It is easy to see why "true dreamers," people gifted with the ability to foresee events in dreams, were considered in league with the devil in olden times. Mrs. G. had a rather unusual dream one night about a fire in the living room and the strange thing about that fire was that it ran up the wall. The following day she happened to be talking to her neighbor, Jean, and her neighbor's mother, and she mentioned the unusual dream she had had the previous evening. The mother gave Mrs. G. a terrified look and ran away. The neighbor explained that earlier that morning her little boy had started a fire in the living room which caught on the curtains and did indeed run up the wall. Fortunately, they were able to put it out in time. There was no way in which Mrs. G. could have had prior knowledge of this event.

Dr. Calvin Hall states, in discussing the meaning of dreams, "Dreams are purely and simply hallucinations." He goes on to explain that a hallucination is an event that isn't really taking place, and that "dreams are creative expressions of the human mind," again intimating that for some reason or other we manufacture our own dreams, that dreams are the product of humans. Dr. Hall, of course, has made no allowances for psychic dreams. He goes to great lengths to explain seemingly psychic dreams as expressions of human longings, needs, problems and so forth. But he doesn't explain how it is possible for dreamers to obtain exact knowledge of future events, details of which are not even in existence at the time of the dream.

One of the largest German newspapers is currently upsetting the apple cart of conventional beliefs with a series dealing with "second sight." Among the examples in this newspaper series is the story of actress Christine Mylius, who has dreamt true since age twelve. At that time she had a dream in which she saw her elder sister on the water but somehow in the Alps as well. Three weeks later her sister drowned in a mountain lake in Bavaria. Since that time Mrs. Mylius has registered a total of 2,439 dreams with Professor Hans Bender of the Freiburg Institute of Parapsychology. Her "dream journal," containing 200 pages of prophetic dreams, has just been published in Germany. These dreams contain correctly predicted traffic accidents involving her mother and her son, various suicides of friends and relatives and material pertaining to total strangers which nevertheless turned out to be true in the end. Mrs. Mylius also was very good with newspaper headlines long before the events took shape and of course long before the printer actually set type for the headlines of which she dreamt. On January 4, 1967, she correctly foretold and registered with Dr. Bender the headline pertaining to the *Apollo* catastrophe of January 27, 1967. The German dreamer notes that her most evidential dreams occurred to her when she was under emotional stress or pressure. With the realization of the dream material and her registration of it, the tension left her.

All kinds of people have "true dreams," that is to say, dreams that later come true. The ability spans every conceivable class of people, and there is absolutely no way of narrowing it down to any specific group of individuals. If anything, one might say that people who have no strong prejudices against ESP and who live fairly harmonious lives are more likely to have psychic dreams than others not so inclined. The difficulty with individuals undergoing psychiatric treatment or possessed of strong obstructionist views on the subject is that they would either tend to embellish dream material on reporting it or suppress it. A very fine example of a well-balanced individual who has shown an increasing amount of ESP is the artist Ingrid B., with whom I have worked on many occasions, investigating cases or experimenting with various forms of psychometry.

On March 8, 1972, Ingrid reported to me a dream she had had on February 29, 1972. "I had a dream concerning a man at work. I dreamt he came into my office, was wearing a plaid sports jacket and turtleneck sweater and said, 'How are you?' and 'We must get together for a drink sometime.' The next morning the same friend did come into my office wearing the exact clothes I had seen him wear and he said, 'How are you?' followed by, 'We haven't talked in a while so we have to get together sometime.' Except for the slight variation in the last line, the dream was completely exact." Since Ingrid's dream occurred only a day before the actual happening, one might conceivably assume that the thoughts of the event were already embedded in the unconscious mind of her friend. But there are difficulties with that explanation. While it might hold water for the clothes seen in the dream and actually worn by the man in real life, the choice of words could not have been preplanned, even if the man had intended to visit with the artist.

Ingrid reported another dream, which occurred on January 29, 1973. In the dream she saw a girl friend she had not seen for almost a year. Ingrid was returning to her home on Staten Island from the city, and as she was walking along Battery Park, she saw her friend coming the other way. It was springtime, and the girl looked thinner and better than she had ever seen her look. Ingrid noticed that her friend was wearing an antique white dress with embroidery on the front. Behind her lagged a tall, thin young man with sandy hair. He was wearing dark slacks and a white shirt with rolled-up sleeves and an open collar. He looked rather bored. As Ingrid passed her friend, she called out to her but her friend stuck up her nose and said, "Who needs you anyway?" The dream seemed so unusual to Ingrid that she decided to call her girl friend to check on its contents. Her friend confirmed that she had been thinking of Ingrid the night before. Also that she had lately lost twelve pounds and had stopped seeing a steady boyfriend. The boyfriend she described as tall, with sandy hair and wearing the clothes Ingrid saw him wear in her dream. As to the white dress which to Ingrid looked like an antique nightgown, her friend confirmed that she owned such a gown but that it had been in storage with her mother. At the time Ingrid was having her dream, she was thinking of getting it back. From this it would appear that Ingrid, in the dream state, was able to tune in on her friend's thoughts and permit her own unconscious mind to report them to her conscious mind to be sorted out, and eventually take some sort of action, which she did by calling her friend.

A third dream reported by Ingrid seems also worth mentioning here. In September of 1974, Ingrid and her fiancé had been thinking of buying an antique sofa, but could not find the right one. On September 10, 1974, Ingrid dreamt that she and her fiancé went into the country and stopped the car in front of a house where they saw a woman wearing a simple housedress. The house had a door in the center, there was a very peaked roof and as the woman, in the dream, stepped onto the lawn, she said, "I have something for you." The dream was so vivid that Ingrid decided it had significance for the future. On a hunch, she decided to follow up on an ad she had previously seen in *Antiques Magazine*, telephoned the advertiser and discovered that this dealer did indeed have a sofa which looked like the one they were looking for. Under the circumstances, they decided to drive up that same weekend. "As we drove up to the house it appeared just as I had seen it in the dream. It was an eighteenth-century farmhouse with a door in the center of the eaves and the reason for the peaked roof was that it was actually a side entrance from the road. The woman was a simple lady wearing a flowered sort of housedress and I did buy the sofa."

Mrs. Susannah D. of New Jersey is a housewife who has had evidential dreams since age twenty. After her marriage she lived for a time at Lake Worth, Florida, but three months later the family decided to come back to New Jersey. The night before they were ready to leave, Mrs. D. had a dream. She saw a woman dressed all in black standing beside a car turned upside down, dabbing at her eyes with a white handkerchief. In the dream, the woman said to Mrs. D., "Please find my daughter, tell my daughter." Mrs. D. remembered clearly thinking in the dream that she forgot to ask the stranger for the name of that daughter, so how could she tell her? The following morning Mrs. D. told her husband of the dream and begged him not to leave that morning. She felt it was a sure sign from fate that they would have an accident. But her husband became irritated at the thought of delay and insisted that they leave as planned. They weren't out of the state of Florida yet when upon rounding a curve they noticed a long line of cars and police cars rushing by. They stopped, and looked to see what was the matter. Down in a gully was a car upside down, and a woman dressed all in black standing alongside, crying. Mrs. D. got out of her car and inquired what had happened. She was informed that the woman's daughter had been killed and was still trapped in the car.

Again, the dream content nearly fits the actual event, except that the information about the dead daughter was obtained from witnesses rather than from the woman in black herself. Nevertheless, this type of dream clearly shows that some individuals can tune in on future events before these events have become objective reality.

Specialist Fourth Class David P. had a dream which came true on *two* separate occasions. At age ten he dreamt that he was running on a lighted path, running from the lighted path into darkness. Now, such a dream can easily be explained as symbolic or of psychoanalytical significance. But young David went into the Boy Scouts and in his second year, in 1965, found himself at a summer camp. Coming back from a campfire one night, he had exactly the same experience as he had dreamt several years before, trying to catch up with the rest of his friends. The moon shone down as he ran on the path and the scene was exactly what he had seen in his dream. But then in February of 1972, when he was in the Army, he found himself in exactly the same situation again—the scene he had seen in his dream.

Mrs. Sandra M. is on active military duty with the Air Force, as is her husband. He works as an aircraft mechanic and she is a computer operator and both are twenty-five years of age. Mrs. M. has had several veridical dreams. One that was particularly interesting occurred to her in July of 1970, when she and her husband were stationed at Travis Air Force Base in California. Their best friends at the base were named Darlene and Reuben, the latter stationed in Vietnam and at the time not due back for another six months. In this particular dream Mrs. M. had the impression that Reuben was coming home soon but that when he got to the base he could not find Darlene. He looked and looked for her but then left because he could not wait. Mrs. M. reported this dream to her husband upon awakening and later in the day also to her friend. It seemed an unlikely dream since Darlene hardly ever went anywhere, so the likelihood of her husband returning and not being able to find her was indeed remote. A month later Reuben came home on an emergency leave, unexpectedly, and when he got to Travis Air Force Base he could not find Darlene. So he left a note and went on to Santa Monica, where his grandmother was dying. Even though Darlene normally stayed around the house, that particular time she had gone square dancing and did not return home until after midnight.

Another interesting dream concerned a future assignment for Mr. and Mrs. M. In May 1971, she dreamt that she and her husband would be assigned to Robins Air Force Base in Georgia. At the time there were literally thousands of possible bases for them to be sent to, so it was not a question of informed guessing. In October of the same year, her husband's orders came through and they were indeed going to Robins Air Force Base in Georgia. At the time when she had had the dream, *even the Air Force did not know where to send them.*

These two dreams and others by Sergeant Sandra M. are attested to by her friends, and her service supervisor, so there is no doubt as to the authenticity of the reported material and the timing of it. A common criticism of dream material that later comes true is that people do not recall having dreamt certain things until *after* the event takes place: in this case and many others which I am about to report in this book, such a criticism would indeed be without foundation.

Frequently, events which come true at a later date cast a shadow ahead of them, and become known to individuals who have nothing whatsoever to do with the events themselves. Why this is so, and why certain individuals can thus tune in on future events which do not concern them personally, is hard to figure out. But there is an overwhelming body of evidence that it occurs, sometimes frightening the dreamer, sometimes merely puzzling him or her.

Mrs. Elaine F. of Chambersburg, Pennsylvania, had a dream in 1969, in which she saw a group of people having a party. They seemed like girl scouts to her and she herself was off in the trees looking on, while the group was celebrating. Suddenly some people came out of nowhere and began killing the "girl scouts." The killers were dressed in black and had bushy hair. In the dream she was particularly frightened by the eyes of the leader, whom she saw clearly. When she awoke the following morning, she described the scene and how she had seen blood running from the wounds of the victims. Ten days later the Sharon Tate murders broke into the headlines. As soon as Mrs. F. saw a picture of Charles Manson in the newspapers, she recognized him as the man she had seen in her dream earlier.

E. W. is in his late thirties, a chemistry

graduate now working in another field. In January 1958 he was living in Florida with his parents, running a business with them. One night he had a dream in which he became aware of himself taking a shower, when the telephone rang. He waited a few moments to see whether his parents would pick up the phone, since they were usually up early, but since it continued to ring Mr. W. grabbed his robe and answered the telephone. In the dream he noticed that he ran to an upstairs extension in a room which was made up as if no one had slept in it for several days. He grabbed the receiver, which was on a small table next to the bed, and said hello. His mother's voice was on the other end saying, "Son, I am at the hospital with Daddy. He's dying. You'd better call the priest and get here as quickly as possible." And suddenly the strange dream ended and Mr. W. found himself wide awake in bed. He worried about the content of this dream, but decided not to mention it to his parents. At that time his father, seventy-three, was in perfect health and there was no reason why he should be in a hospital.

The dream occurred in January 1958. In late April Mr. W. noticed that his father seemed to have difficulty speaking. Eventually he took him to a doctor and it was thought that Mr. W., Sr., had had a stroke. But the diagnosis seemed uncertain, so Mr. W. took his father to a brain specialist in a larger city. There it was discovered that Mr. W., Sr. had cancer of the brain which was inoperable. They decided to drive back to Florida since there was nothing they could do about it. On the morning of July 15 of the same year, Mr. W. got up fairly early and jumped into the shower. He was just drying himself off when the phone began ringing insistently. He grabbed his bathrobe and answered the phone immediately whereas in the dream he had allowed it to ring for some time! His mother was on the other end of the line, saying the exact words he had heard her say in the dream many months before. "Son, I am at the hospital with Daddy. He's dying. You'd better call the priest and get here as quickly as possible."

Mrs. S. of South Bend, Indiana, had a strange feeling she should visit her grandfather, then living a hundred and twenty miles away in another town. One night she had a dream in which she saw herself in a house she had previously lived in. Her three sisters each had received a letter from a "Bert" but she hadn't gotten one. Next she saw people dressed in black standing around a grave. That was the entire dream, but the following morning her sister called and said that their grandfather had passed away the night before. His nickname had been "Bert."

Charles T. Glover, Jr., a native of Long Island, fifty-two years old, worked in advertising and publishing for ten years, and currently owns his own business as an antique restorer in Oregon. He has had a number of paranormal dreams through the years. Because of that he began to write down his dreams on the chance that some of them might later become reality. One such dream was as follows: he was riding on a train which, as it approached a city, went underground and finally came to stop beside a long, underground platform. He got off the train and walked along the platform with a large crowd of people. Ahead of him, in the distance, he could see a flight of stairs at the end of which shone the light of the outdoors. He went up the stairs and saw before him a roofed-over platform stretching into the distance with railroad tracks on both sides. On his right, in the dream, he could see a large city stretching to the horizon; but on his left he saw complete devastation—nothing but piles of shattered buildings and rubble. Then he awakened and recorded his dream. About a year later, in September of 1942, he went into the armed services and served in New Guinea, the Philippines and ultimately in Japan, where he arrived in September, 1945, and was stationed in a small town called Zushi, about thirty miles south of Tokyo. On his first weekend pass he decided to take the train to Tokyo. As he approached the city, the train dipped underground and finally came to a stop beside a long underground platform. As he joined the horde of people going toward a flight of stairs in the distance and finally began to climb the stairs, he had a strong feeling of *déjà vu*. When he arrived at the roofed-over platform he recalled his dream in vivid detail. On his right stood the intact portion of Tokyo; and on his left were the results of many months of precision bombing by American bombers, aimed at the industrial sections of Tokyo—devastated right up to the railroad tracks.

Another dream seems worthy of being recorded here. In the summer of 1958 Mr. Glover dreamt he was sleeping in a tent beside a stream along with several other people in tents, sleeping bags and trailers. Behind the campsite was a tall, rocky cliff towering over the sleeping campers. Suddenly the earth began to shake and with a tremendous roar a great section of the cliff collapsed and came crashing down on them, burying them all in tons of rock and dirt. Mr. Glover related the dream in every detail to a friend also interested in paranormal dreams, Flora G. of San Francisco. Three days later the newspapers were full of an earth upheaval at Yosemite National Park. A campsite was buried by the very landslide he had vividly seen in his dream.

It is interesting to note that dreams, like other psychic impressions, sometimes reverse left and right or up and down, though not always. There is a very old tradition that one can enter the world of magic by stepping through a mirror, and that a mirror is in fact the borderline between the world of reality and imagination. It is of course a fact that our retina sees things upside down and straightens them up before forwarding the impression to the brain centers dealing with sight. In other words, we see the world upside down, but perceive it as right side up.

I am indebted to Mrs. Dixie B. of Winston-Salem, North Carolina, for the account of a friend, choreographer Peter Van Muyden. The two belonged to an experimental group that had been practicing meditation and various forms of consciousness expansion under the direction of Pastor George Colgin of the local Baptist church.

The dream which Mr. Van Muyden reported was the following: when he was a young man in Holland, he had the same dream several times. He saw a castle with a "freeway" in front of it and a river flowing beside. In the dream, he went through the gates, through a rose garden and into the castle. On the right he observed a stairway and in the middle of the stairs he saw an old woman. He went past her and saw two doors. He opened the door on the right and saw a room papered with Bordeaux red wallpaper, and a man hanging.

The dream made no sense to him at the time but many years later, by chance, he visited a castle and recognized it as the one of his dreams. There was the freeway in front, the river at the side, and the gates were the same, except that the position of the rose garden was reversed, as if seen through a mirror. When he entered the front door, the stairway was on the left. An old woman, the owner's aunt, did live there. He went up the stairs and since the garden stairway had been reversed from what he had seen in his dream, he decided to try the doorway on the left instead of on the right, and found it locked, but when he asked if he could see the room, he was told that the owner's aunt preferred to have it locked. It seems that the contractor who had renovated the castle had hanged himself in that room. When the room was finally opened to Mr. Van Muyden, he saw that it was indeed covered by the Bordeaux red wallpaper he had seen in his dream.

Now, the interesting thing about this dream is that the dreamer not only foresaw a future event before he had knowledge of it or before he had any contact with those who would eventually lead him to the place where the event would occur, but it even includes a tragedy, the contractor's suicide, which is subject to a number of imponderables. Nevertheless, the contractor hanged himself, and the dream became reality many years after the dreamer had perceived it.

Dreams of this kind seem to indicate an almost fatalistic sequence of events, even covering the seemingly free will and actions of other individuals totally unconnected with the dreamer!

Probably the least likely group of professionals to accept psychic material as true are magicians and other illusionists. There are a few notable exceptions where magicians have had experiences themselves which they cannot explain away. Such is the case of Barrie Schlenker, who works under the professional name of Vincent Barrett, and who makes his home in Lehighton, Pennsylvania. Billed as the man with the X-ray eyes, young Barrett presents a program of mentalist feats, which are frankly termed stunts and do not involve any kind of psychic ability. Nevertheless, on the morning of March 10, 1964, while he was living at home with his mother and grandmother, he had a dream early in the morning which he recorded upon awakening.

"The dream was one of those very vivid ones

which seemed so very real at the time. I was dreaming that for a reason unknown to me I was driving my car in my bathrobe and pajamas. I didn't know where I was going, perhaps if I would have been allowed to finish the dream I would have found out, but I was suddenly awakened by the sound of a bell ringing with some strange note of urgency. I knew immediately what I was hearing: my grandmother had been ill for several years, she had had several strokes and many bad heart spells during that time, and I had built a bell pull system in our house so that if she needed help at any time she could pull a cord in any room of the house and a bell would ring in the stairwell loud enough for anyone else in the house to hear. This was the bell I heard on the morning of March 10, 1964. I got up as quickly as I could out of a sound sleep and went downstairs to see what was the matter. My mother and grandmother had gotten up about an hour earlier, had breakfast together and had been washing their breakfast dishes when my grandmother had suffered another heart spell. She sat down on a chair in the kitchen, never to get up again. Mother ran to the bell rope and rang it violently to wake me, which it did. As I ran downstairs I could see my grandmother propped up on the kitchen chair and I knew what had happened. My mother said I should quickly call the doctor and then go out in the country to get my aunt, mother's sister. I made the phone call and then without taking time to dress, just putting a coat over my shoulders on top of my bathrobe and pajamas, I got into my car and drove away, just then remembering my dream of only a few moments ago."

Dreams are by no means always harbingers of important events, nor do they necessarily contain messages of vital significance. In fact, the majority of dreams seem rather unimportant in the long view since they pertain to relatively unimportant matters. One wonders why the "powers that be" bother to allow people a glance into the future in such trifling matters. The answer, of course, is obvious: paranormal dreams are subject to laws just like everything else in nature. They are not the whim of individuals, even those on the Other Side of life. If an individual has the gift of psychic dreams, whatever material impresses itself on his or her unconscious mind at the time will be received and remembered upon awakening, whether it is important or not. There is no such thing as selective dreaming in this category of dream material, i.e., material pertaining to the so-called future. Though there is direction in some form of paranormal dreams.

I could go on and on with material of this kind, all of it verified, all of it told to witnesses prior to the event taking place in reality. But I think the evidence is overwhelming as it stands. In summing up this category, prophetic dreams, it appears to me that they cannot be forced to occur at will, that they are not directional in the sense other categories of dreams are, but much more haphazard, as if the precognitive contact were made at random, regardless of importance, regardless of the dreamer's own needs or connections. We must therefore seek an explanation for this ability to dream true in the mechanics of dreaming itself. Something occurs in the makeup of the dreamer's personality during sleep which allows his or her unconscious mind to tune in on the future events recorded in the dream. It may be that the area covered by the dreamer is linked to geographical concepts, or to intensity concepts, or to some other form of attraction. For the present, let us be satisfied to state that prophetic dreams are fairly common, cannot be regulated in any way, but can be verified and should, as a matter of fact, always be told on arising to competent witnesses.

# REINCARNATION DREAMS

*(The Psychic Side of Dreams)*

This is the stuff that some commercial novels are made of: recurrent dreams of previous lives, usually very colorful, which keep on recurring and puzzling the dreamer. Unfortunately, not all reincarnation dreams are as precise or as insistent. The majority of this type of dream is partial, fragmentary, hazy and altogether frustrating in that it leaves the dreamer with the feeling of having been given some sort of unusual glance at his or her own past without spelling it out so one could go to the nearest library and look it all up.

Reincarnation dreams are dreams in which the individual sees him or herself going through actions or in places with which he or she is not familiar in conscious existence. They differ from the first two categories of dreams in precisely the same areas in which all psychic dreams differ from "ordinary" dreams, by being specific and, even when fragmentary, sharp and fully remembered upon awakening. In particular, reincarnation dreams have a habit of coming in series, usually exact repetitions of one dream, more rarely partial repetition with follow-ups. An often asked question with this type of dream is whether it may be due to clairvoyance—a discarnate's attempt to communicate to the dreamer his or her story. This argument is easily dismissed: those who have reincarnation dreams are rarely, if ever, psychic before or after the occurrence of such dreams and have shown no particular talents with ESP in other areas. Also, true reincarnation dreams leave a residue of restlessness, a compulsion to do something about the dream that is not present with other types of dreams. In the dream, the dreamer sees himself looking different from his present appearance and yet he knows that it is himself and it is to him all these things are happening. With other types of psychic dreams, a scene is seen but the dreamer himself is the observer, not the participant, except of course with dreams pertaining to the future, in which an event that has not yet come to pass is being shown to the dreamer. In that case he may appear in the dream as his present self, looking exactly as he does when he goes to bed. But reincarnation dreams always deal with the past, therefore the dreamer never looks the way he does in his present life.

Conventional psychiatrists may dismiss such dreams as fantasies, wish-fulfillment dreams, meaningless romanticizing of present-day events, and altogether connected with the personality of the dreamer without containing so much as an ounce of information from the dreamer's earlier lives. They do not accept reincarnation as a valid theory. But it is difficult to explain by such criteria the number of verified reincarnation dreams on record. When the dreamer remembers upon awakening a dream in which he saw himself as a different person in a different age, when he remembers names, data and circumstances from the past with which he is not familiar in his present life, and to which he has no access, if he wanted to research it, and when such material is subsequently proven to be authentic, and the personality referred to by the dreamer actually existed, then it is very difficult indeed to blame it all on the personality quirks of the *present* person.

Reincarnation memories come to some people at various times in their lives, but the majority of us never have them. It is my conviction from the studies I have undertaken, that only where a previous lifetime has in some way been cut short or has been tragic, is the individual given part of the memory as a sort of bonus to influence his or her present conduct. The lives of people who have had full lives prior to the present one are never remembered, neither in dreams nor in so-called waking flashes or in *déjà vu*, which is a phenomenon sometimes related to reincarnation memories. Most *déjà vu* is simply precognitive experiences which are not realized at the time they occur but are remembered when the precognitive experience becomes objective reality. Some *déjà vu*, especially that which is more involved and contains precise and detailed information about places and situations the perceiver is not familiar with, is due to reincarnation memories. All *déjà vu* occurs in the waking state and is therefore not properly within the scope of this work, but it is related to reincarnation dreams, in that it also discloses to the individual some hidden material from his or her own past.

With the flood of interesting dreams occurring to people all over the world, we must guard against overenthusiasm when it comes to potential reincarnation material. To begin with, only recurrent dreams need be considered here. That is, dreams that occur to the dreamer a number of times in repetitive fashion, and that contain more or less the same material. I have found that reincarnation material forces itself on the unconscious mind of the sleeper, perhaps because it wants to be acknowledged so that the lessons of a previous lifetime may be applied to the present. Together with waking flashes of prior life memories, recurrent dreams form the bulk of material where hypnosis may be of practical use. Through a method called hypnotic regression, the individual is taken back first to his or her own childhood and then gradually to the threshold of birth, and beyond it into a presumed earlier lifetime. This is done in stages and success depends upon the ability of the subject to go into the hypnotic state. If successful, it will result in loosening the memory and allow the subject to relate his or her earlier experiences freely and to describe the scenes from previous lives in greater detail than was possible in the recurrent dreams. Also, the hypnotherapist can excise unpleasant memories from previous lifetimes at the same time, while bringing to the surface details of such lives which may be checked out in conventional records.

I have undertaken this type of regression many times with suitable subjects, but never with anyone who simply wanted to be regressed in order to find out who he or she might have been in a previous life. Not only do I feel that such attempts are bound to fail and would not produce any information, but I find such attempts morally objectionable because it seems to me that reincarnation memories occur to people to whom they *ought to* occur and not to others. In artificially ferreting out such hidden material, might we not hurt the individual's karmic progress? In a previous book, entitled *Born Again*, I reported some of the extraordinary dreams of a number of subjects that proved to be authentic material from past lives. Since then, new cases have come to my attention, proving that reincarnation dreams are not altogether rare.

Where then does one draw the line between fantasy dreams and material capable of verification? As with all dreams, we must take into account the individual's background, education, ability to involve him or herself with the subject of his or her dreams, and other personal factors which differ from individual to individual. Let us assume that someone dreams of a life in ancient Egypt, but has a working knowledge of Egyptology, or perhaps a personal interest in the field. Then we must look at such dreams with the jaundiced eye of the doubter: was the dream material suggested by conscious knowledge of the dreamer, flushed out as cleverly as the unconscious is able to, or are we dealing here with reincarnation? Are memories of life in ancient Egypt *causing* the dreamer to pursue a study of that period in his or her current life?

It is important to determine what came first, the dream or the interest in the subject matter. Anyone judging the veridicality of reincarnation dreams without personally being familiar with the subject or at the very least with a full transcript of the dreams and the background of the dreamer, will not arrive at any fair conclusion concerning the authenticity of such material. Opinions are not facts.

Karen G. is in her middle twenties, a member of the United States Air Force, stationed abroad. She has had three recurrent dreams which have remained with her vividly and disturbingly. Her husband, unfortunately, puts no stock in such material, so Mrs. G. contacted me to put it on record. When she was twenty-one she dreamt of a woman in a long, dark dress and a white apron—a good-looking woman with long black hair and green eyes. People full of hatred were shouting at her and tying her to a tree. They put brush under her feet and kept yelling, "Burn her, burn the witch!" She cried that she was not a witch and that if she were they would never have had a chance to burn her. "When she said that, I suddenly realized with quite a shock that I was this girl. I was watching this in full color and I somehow knew that I was her," Mrs. G. explained.

The woman in Mrs. G.'s dream tried to make people understand that she "just knew things," and that was all. When they wouldn't listen, she called them fools. Then the people lit the fire. It was horrible to the dreamer because she knew that she was innocent, she knew she was trying to get through to them. "I felt the heat of the fire and knew her anguish one last time, that they were wrong and someday they would know it."

Mrs. G. did not get any details, although for some reason the names Elizabeth and Suzanne come to her mind in connection with this dream. She has never been able to forget it and it has troubled her a great deal; she has dreamt it at least three times.

The second dream was about another woman, who was dressed in a long dress. Somehow Mrs. G. knew this was in France. The woman was at a party in a large mansion and the dreamer knew that she was either the wife or mistress of the man who owned the mansion. In the dream she saw a game being played, where one person was sent from the room while the others hid. When the person came back he was blind-folded. In this scene it was the owner of the mansion and he had to look for the woman. While he was feeling his way around the room looking for her, the others moved the furniture around to confuse him. He thought it was fun at first, but then he began to get angry and the woman got scared. "That is when I knew I was her. I ran and hid in a closet. Then the dream switched to a little town and the woman was arguing with a man and he said if she continued to keep doing something he would take their baby away from her. She then got hysterical and threatened to commit suicide. Then the dream switched back to the mansion again, showing her crying and pleading with this man. She then opened the French doors, ran out on the balcony and jumped off." That was the end of the dream.

Mrs. G. dreamt it when she was twenty-one and again about a year later, at which time she suddenly felt inside that the man of this dream was now the man she worked for.

(It is not unusual for people with reincarnation dreams to feel that certain individuals now living may be reincarnated from the same period as the dream. Usually, people the dreamer has known in a past life are now in a different position and usually quite unaware of the connection. It is of course difficult to prove this unless they also have recurrent dreams or some form of recognition that a previous lifetime has connected them with that person.)

The third dream which so disturbed Mrs. G. was rather short. She saw a woman and a child, and it seems that a volcano had erupted and the lava was coming down all around them. All the woman could think of was to save the child; she grabbed it and ran as fast as she could up a path and finally made it to a place which looked like a city or village built into a mountain; the windows were protected by sliding glass. "I remember a feeling of relief when they went inside and stood watching the lava come down. In the last part of the dream the whole place began to rumble and shake."

Now, the interesting thing about these three

dreams is that they have one thing in common (that is, if the third dream also leads to sudden death). In the first dream, Mrs. G. is a witch burned at the stake, in the second she jumps to her death, and in the third she is a victim of a natural catastrophe—all three lives cut short by *external forces*.

Mrs. Shirley F. of Denver, Colorado, has had a number of recurrent dreams over the past twenty-five years. She sees a large castle, always the same one, but a different room each time. She cannot make out the location of this castle but knows that it is situated on a cliff in rugged terrain and overlooks an ocean. In the dreams, she is always strolling through it leisurely, at times looking for someone, but always with the feeling of being at home.

On the surface of it, one might say that dreaming of a castle, especially if one is in modest circumstances, is simply another form of romantic wish fulflllment. But this need not be so: a large percentage of the European population lived in some form of mansion or castle, not necessarily as the owner, and if this recurrent dream refers to the Middle Ages or a period prior to, let us say 1800, dreaming of a castle as home is not altogether unusual. Unfortunately, with so little to go on, there is no way in which an identity in a previous lifetime can be proven.

Chris Roberts, thirty years old, was working toward his bachelor's degree in social case work, when he first contacted me in 1970. The young man has had a number of experiences which lead him to believe that he has lived before, perhaps several times. One particular dream incident stands out. When he was working at a private, non-profit rehabilitation center in upstate New York, he met a young woman named Josephine F. Instantly on meeting, they recognized each other as if they had known each other before, which in fact they had not. As time went on they have come to realize a mutual former existence, perhaps as husband and wife, in Japan at some previous time. Even though Miss F. is Italian, she looks to Mr. Roberts astonishingly oriental, and his daily living habits are also somewhat oriental.

One night, while many miles apart, both individuals dreamt the identical dream at the same time, and related it to each other the following day, Miss F. starting at the beginning, and Mr. Roberts coming in at the middle and telling it to the end, much to their mutual amazement. They dreamt of some natural catastrophe in earlier times, during which they were both thrown into the sea. They remember swimming in a tumultuous sea, surrounded by other struggling survivors until they were somehow able to crawl inside a floating house. From a window in the house, they were able to watch the approaching onslaught of a great wave that finally engulfed and drowned them both.

Not all reincarnation dreams are clearly defined, with a beginning, middle, and end; sometimes the end is left in doubt. Also, occasionally symbolic dream material pertaining to the present lifetime becomes intermingled with reincarnation dreams and confuses the issue. Such material is particularly hard to interpret.

Claudia L. lives in Michigan, is in her late twenties and had a recurrent dream from the time she was five years old until she turned thirteen. In this dream she was always a child of about five years. She and her mother had gone into a tall building which she compared to a skyscraper. Her mother, and another adult who appeared in the dream, had left her alone while they went to a business appointment in the building and somehow the little girl got separated from them. She did not miss her companions but wandered around the great, vaulted reception area, noticing colored shop windows, flowers and a variety of people. Among the decorations there were some tall jars, large enough for her to jump into. As she wandered about she realized that the building was deserted, as if she had gotten trapped inside it after working hours, and then she heard someone approaching down a hallway. She thought it was a night watchman coming to see what she was doing. But the man appeared to be wearing a coat of mail. He came after the little girl in a menacing way, and she started to run. She was afraid, in the dream, that she was going to be stabbed to death with the man's lance, but then she managed to lose him by jumping into one of the large jars. He went clanking by, and at this point there was a blotting out of the dream.

Miss L. does not know whether the pot was

smashed and she was found, or whether she had managed to fool her pursuer. On awakening, however, she always felt that she had left something unfinished or left someone behind. Because of the seeming absurdity of a mail-clad night watchman pursuing her in what appeared to be a modern building, Miss L. dared not mention the dream to anyone lest she be ridiculed. But why was the dream recurring to her, and why was she unsettled by its content? Could it not be that the tall building or perhaps the watchman's coat of mail was an interposition from another type dream?

Dreams shared by more than one person are much rarer than single dreams.

Richard U. of New York State in 1970 dreamt of a very strange scene. In the dream he was astride a horse on a beach, waiting for a ship. There was a group of men with him, dressed in what he later realized was armor like that worn by the crusaders. The water seemed very blue and crystal clear.

The following day he mentioned this dream to two close friends. It then developed that both had dreamt of being on an old ship. They were dressed in flowing robes, heading for an island, and they, too, had been impressed with the crystal clear blue water. Had the three of them seen the same scene from a different point of view, because they had been in it together in a previous lifetime?

Mrs. Georgia G. has always felt that she once lived in the Old West, that is, in another lifetime.

Right now, she lives in Iowa, is in her early thirties, married for the second time, and the mother of two children. Her background is English and German, as it is with many of the people in her part of the Middle West.

The first dream which made her wonder about having lived before happened to her rather unexpectedly. The scene showed a beautiful summer day, and it was either noon or very early afternoon since the sun was shining overhead. She saw a town square with one side bordered by a huge, long stone wall; the center of the town square seemed shaded. There were two padres standing there looking down on a young woman who was kneeling before them. Georgia could not see their faces since they were in the shaded area, but the woman seemed to be around thirty years old and had on drab, dark clothes. There was a crowd of people at the end of the wall in the distance, cowering away from the middle of the square where these three figures were. The woman, speaking in English, said, "I beg of you, have mercy on me." She was pleading with the two priests but they only watched her in stony silence. All at once she knew she was that woman! She looked at the crowd in the distance but could see they didn't want to get mixed up in the affair, whatever it was.

Although the dream occurred to her only once, it was of such clarity and power that she could not forget it afterward. Also, she remembered that when she was a child, her parents had the greatest difficulty getting her to go to Sunday school. She would pretend that she was sick in order to get out of having to go, and even now she does not go to church. Had she been made to suffer in a previous lifetime because of psychic ability? From her description, the two padres may have been eighteenth—or early nineteenth-century priests, in what was then the Spanish part of North America. Unfortunately, her dream cannot be pinpointed any further, but to her it is like a corridor to another lifetime.

There are many cases on record of dreams relating to previous incarnations, but dreams relating to the "transitional period," or the very moment of "coming back" are very rare indeed. Perhaps this is so because according to karmic law that is one part of the experience one is not supposed to remember. At any rate, I have reported some of these instances in *Born Again*, where the process of forgetting one lifetime and being made ready for another is described. There is mention of a "well of forgetfulness," the water of which accomplishes this remarkable feat.

Mrs. P. L. is a divorced woman in her early fifties who lives in the South. Her studies included three years of pre-med, and at one time she taught at a secretarial school. Mrs. L. dreams in color, and in French and Hebrew, languages she neither speaks nor understands. But the dream that interested me most occurred to her in 1938.

She dreamt that she went into a circular enclosure with a fountain in the center. There were small cubicles covered with curtains and she was told to go into one of them to "receive." Inside was a water pipe which she smoked until she lost consciousness. When she awoke the following morning, she was in a stupor for over an hour, something very unusual for her. Had she had a glimpse at the "machine" used by the powers that be to make people forget their previous life experiences, in order to be properly prepared for the next one?

There are many valid techniques of reinforcing one's ability to remember dreams upon awakening, if that is necessary. I find that on the whole true psychic dreams do not require much reinforcing because they are rarely forgotten, certainly not quickly. Nevertheless, there may be people who for one or another reason are unable to recall more than a fragment of unusual dreams.

Just as waking flashes of previous lives may be triggered by actually passing through a place where one has lived before, or by meeting someone whom one instinctively feels one has known before, so dreams of this type can be triggered by external, realistic experiences prior to sleep.

For instance, someone may pass through a strange town, which he does not know consciously. At night, he has a reincarnation dream in which he finds himself in the same place, but in an earlier age. In such a case the dream was triggered by his actual passing through the town, although he did not receive any impression of previous experiences while awake.

These experiences differ from person to person and have a lot to do with the individual and his or her makeup. In some, reincarnation material finds it easier to get to the surface than in others, and it is entirely conceivable that material of this nature can lie dormant for many years until an external event brings it to the surface or triggers its appearance in the dream state. Much of the material of this kind is fragmentary and no more than a flash or a small portion of a previous existence. When there is unfinished business, so to speak, and the person is to receive a detailed message which will help him or her cope better with his present existence, the reincarnation dream is longer and far more detailed than these common sudden flashes or one-time memories.

When I said earlier that recurrent dreams are a sign of reincarnation memories, I did not mean to exclude single dreams of this nature. They, too, can have reincarnation content, but it is my experience with the material with which I am familiar, that in the majority of cases, if not all, additional material comes to the surface sooner or later. Even when dreams are not recurrent or parallel, there may be dreams connected with each other, or dreams dreamt in part at various times in a person's present life. A great deal of reincarnation material manifests itself in hunches or strange attractions to places and people, which are hard to verbalize or even rationalize. Nevertheless, they come from the same source as the more elaborate dreams do. It is my conviction that previous lives imprint themselves upon the psyche of each person, and stay in place when subsequent layers of consciousness are added on top. Thus a so-called "old soul" consists of a substantial numof layers of consciousness. From time to time, the earlier layers of experience protrude or intrude into the present existence, giving information or conveying feelings alien to the person in his or her present circumstances. We are at all times the sum total of our previous lives, even if we fail to remember them in the conscious state.

Lastly, there is a category of reincarnation dream, usually recurrent, which I would like to call *fear dreams*. They have to do with the *manner* in which a person passed on in a previous existence. Because of it, they cast a shadow, so to speak, over the present existence. Sometimes the anxiety ceases abruptly when a certain age is reached, and the dreams stop. In other cases, the dreams represent a problem and may lead to psychological disturbances or maladjustments. In such cases hypnotherapy is indicated. I have hypnotically regressed such people, with the approval of their physicians, when I thought I could excise the fear dream in the process. Of course, all reincarnation memories are due to unfinished lives of one kind or another, but with fear dreams, the manner of death is particularly violent or strongly remembered, more than the rest of the dream, to the point where it may become an obsession with similar circumstances if and when they occur in the present incarnation.

Mrs. Margaret K., age forty, married, mother of three children, native of Mississippi, but currently residing in Kentucky, got in touch with me after she had read *Born Again*. My earlier book gave her the courage to come forward with the startling experiences of her life. "*Born Again* is the most intriguing book I have ever read on reincarnation; never before have I felt such an impulse to write an author," she began.

Mrs. K. has worked at various jobs: secretary, bookkeeper, saleslady, waitress. Beginning when she was a small child of six or seven, she had a recurrent dream until she was well into her teens. In the dream she was on the ground and flames were leaping up from it all around her. But when the flames reached to within a small circle of her, they would come no closer. Next she would find herself in the middle of water. The flames would start from the shoreline and proceed toward her, always stopping before they reached her. She would awaken from these dreams very much disturbed.

Mrs. K. is one of those few who does have ESP, despite her reincarnation dreams. In recent years she had another recurrent dream, about a man connected with the sea. She believes herself to be his wife or sweetheart in the dream, but there is always something keeping them apart. When she awakes from these dreams she feels a deep sense of loss and something like grief. All day long she will remember the man, yet she does not know who he is.

There may be a connection between the two dreams. At any rate, Mrs. K. has had a terrible horror of fire all her life. So far, nothing involving a fire has happened to her in actual life, but she feels that her fear is based upon an earlier existence, with her childhood dream pointing to danger or perhaps death connected with fire.

JoAnne M. lives in Ohio and has never shown any interest in the occult or in reincarnation in particular. Two of her adolescent recurrent dreams have left her with a sense of fear to the point where she is still afraid to be alone in a two-story house at night. She also has a deep-rooted fear of knives.

She started having the first of the two dreams when she was about eight years old. In the dream, she is riding an old-model bike, perhaps the kind that was in use at the turn of the century or shortly thereafter. She sees herself riding in a park that has trees and a stream, and she is going down a hill. When she reaches the bottom of the hill, there is another hill but on the other side of the stream, which has a bridge across it. She crosses the bridge and on top of the second hill, she finds what seems to be a Victorian house, two-storied with many turrets, porches and gables. She dismounts from her bike and leaving it outside, enters the house. At this point in the dream, she always wakes up in terror with the certain knowledge that she was very much afraid inside the house in the dream.

Since she has this dream primarily when she is ill, there might be a connection between the inside of the house and illness.

The other dream she had during her early teens. At the time Mrs. M. and her sister shared a large dormer type bedroom in the attic of a bungalow. At one end of the room were their beds, at the other end the stairs that curved down to the main floor. She would often dream of an old lady ascending some stairs, with a huge knife in her hand and in the dream Mrs. M. knew that she was going to be stabbed. She would wake up terrified and would often lie awake for hours, staring at the stairs, waiting for the woman to come up, and afraid to go to sleep because she knew the woman would come. "I had this dream over and over and I would be terrified, lying in a cold sweat. I never told my mother or anyone else because I was in my teens and embarrassed that they would think I was odd," Mrs. M. explains. When she went on to college, the dream faded and she has never had it since.

But to this day she is afraid of knives, even small paring knives, in another person's hands. And whenever her husband is out of town, she is afraid to sleep alone in their second-story bedroom. She turns on all the lights, brings the dog into the room with her, and it is often early morning before she can finally fall asleep.

June Weidemann, a professional nurse, has long had an active interest in parapsychology. In her case this is not surprising since she has experienced a number of unusual incidents all her life. Again, she is one of the few people who combines ESP ability with some reincarnation dreams.

When June was seven years old she suddenly seemed to "wake up," and had a distinct feeling of being in a strange place with strange people. For a period of about six months she was convinced that her parents were not her parents at all because of their peculiar *round* eyes—which seemed strange to her. Finally, her mother had had enough, and showed her newspaper clippings announcing her birth, and her birth certificate, to convince her that she really was their daughter!

This did indeed convince June, but about that time she had a recurrent dream concerning a household compound in a house in China. All she could ever see was the bare compound laid with large, flat stones and a wall of the same material. In the center grew a tree which sometimes had beautiful blossoms and sometimes was bare and covered lightly with a layer of snow. There was no one else there but herself. At the same time she became aware of a certain perfume that surrounded her. This particular odor would always bring to mind the words "ming tree," although she did not at the time know what ming trees were. The oriental dream is rather comforting to Mrs. Weidemann, and in this life she has grown more and more fond of oriental things.

However, she has had two other recurrent dreams which are more disturbing. In one of them she is a young man with leather britches standing on top of a crude ladder that is leaning against a high wall. It is night; the ground below her falls away from the ladder, and she finds herself slowly falling backward, still holding tightly to the top rung of the ladder. She usually jerks herself awake with this dream, but sometimes, just before she hits the ground, she thinks to herself, still in the dream, "Oh no, not again!" The night is always dark, but there is moonlight or some other source of light, for she can see herself falling away from the wall and finds herself trapped under the ladder on the ground.

In still another dream she sees a house in the distance, and runs toward it, happy that she is home at last. She sees herself going up to a porch and she notices the long glass windows on each side of the door. She enters, but the house is bare. She steps down two steps into a room off the foyer. There she sees a rather dilapidated staircase, and a long room with a bay window to the right. Occasionally, when she has had this dream, she has also seen antique furniture in the room, but mostly she sees a threadbare rug on the floor and an empty room. The dream ends there. She has never been in such a house in this life. The dream does not unduly upset her, as does the first one, where she falls off the ladder, and being a trained nurse and a well-read psychical researcher, Mrs. Weidemann has long since learned to cope with her reincarnation dreams.

# THE EVIDENCE FOR SURVIVAL AFTER DEATH

## *(Beyond This Life)*

Frequently I am asked by doubters: How can one be sure the communication really comes from a dead person and not from the subconscious of the medium? Just as frequently, I am asked in cases in which there is no intermediary involved and the contact is directly between a supposedly dead individual and someone in the physical world, how can one know that the living person is not hallucinating or imagining the whole thing? Finally, how does one know these communications aren't just coincidences?

Some people like to dismiss the facts by blandly claiming that "the majority of ESP experiences can be chalked up to coincidence." It is an all-too-human tendency to resort to pat statements whenever one does not *want* to examine evidence for fear that one's preconceived notions may have to be changed.

When the content of a message is such that it fits only the dead person as originator, and when that communication is with a person who has no possible knowledge of the content beforehand, then we are certainly dealing with psychic phenomenon. It is psychic because the information has been obtained through other means than the ordinary five senses. Has the receiver used his or her own ESP to obtain the information without requiring the presence of a dead communicator on the other end of the line of communication? Has this psychic person somehow drawn from his or her own unconscious or subconscious (pick your term) the very specific message that concerns another person known to be dead? Occasionally this may be possible, though it is by no means likely. But on numerous occasions it simply is impossible. Messages from the dead to the living speak of specific events that have not yet become objective reality to *anyone*.

Later, these events occur and in retrospect the receiver of the message realizes that a dead individual has foreseen them. Or the receiver does not know the personal circumstances of the dead communicator and therefore does not have in his or her own unconscious storehouse the detailed knowledge to draw upon if the message were to originate within him or herself. Time and again, the receiver is taken by surprise and does not expect the contact from the Beyond. There is nothing in his or her thoughts to link the receiver with the dead person. And yet communications of this kind occur with considerable frequency.

Imagining information, if that were possible, will again have to be judged on the truth of the information; if it turns out to be correct and unknown to the receiver at the time of the contact, then it is pretty much a moot question whether he or she "imagined" it psychically or had a genuine communication from the psychic world. Either way it is what we call *paranormal*.

Finally, the word *hallucinating* has been bandied about indiscriminately by would-be parapsychologists explaining phenomena they have not themselves witnessed or investigated. Their aim is to explain these occurrences in terms of "orthodox" science; they forget that science is a *changing* concept.

When a person hallucinates an image or sound, that person is the originator of it and is presumed to have an abnormality of mind or emotional constitution that permits these phenomena to occur. But no one has ever proved that a person manufactures such hallucinations when we are dealing with supposedly "normal," well-adjusted people who do not have a medical history of mental disease or have not partaken of hallucinogenic drugs. *Healthy* people do not hallucinate. In addition, there is a sharp distinction between the phantasms created in the sick mind and those experienced by the healthy as spontaneous experiences. The true hallucinations of mentally sick individuals or of people under the influence of certain drugs are illogical, often monstrous images and symbols far removed from possible reality.

Psychic phenomena, on the other hand, have the ring of truth in them. They seem perfectly logical and well ordered in their sequence of events, and they differ from ordinary life experiences only in that they have not yet occurred or that they are unknown to the recipient at the time they occur.

Coincidence, another term thrown around with abandon by some would-be scientists, is a word requiring further definition. Strictly speaking, it means that events happen in objective reality which are totally unconnected by the common laws of cause and effect, but which somehow *seem* to be connected, while in fact they are not.

Coincidence was a strong argument of the materialistically inclined to deal with the strange links between people that only psychic research can explain in some manner, those weird patterns of fate that defy the laws of cause and effect. Then Carl Jung wrote a fundamental book called *The Law of Meaningful Coincidence or Acasual Synchronicity* in which he painstakingly documented the existence of a second set of laws beyond the common laws of cause and effect. This second set of laws which he called "the laws of meaningful coincidence" do , in his view, connect events and people that are apparently not at all connected in terms of logic. Carl Jung has taken a great deal of wind out of the sails of those who still accept the possibility of "coincidence" in our universe.

I am not one of them. I do not envision any coincidence at all in what appears to be a marvelously well-arranged world where nothing is left to chance. There are connections beyond our understanding, at least our present very limited understanding, but there is nothing in our universe that does not obey *some* set of laws. When the elements of each authenticated case are carefully examined, one realizes that coincidence as a possible explanation is completely out of the question. What we are left with in those cases is the realization that there is no better or alternate explanation than the one that sounds most logical: true contact between the two worlds.

I met Mrs. Claude Thornhill in the winter of 1967 through a mutual friend in the music business, Robert Lissauer, who had known her late bandleader-composer husband. Mrs. Thornhill is a well-read person with a broad educational background who has played an important role in international society. A native of the state of Washington, Ruth Thornhill had her first encounter with the psychic when she was twelve, but it failed to get her particularly interested in the subject, and she took her later experiences in stride, neither rejecting them nor unduly dwelling on them.

Her parents had purchased an old house near Olympia, Washington, and as her uncle and aunt had a house next door to the one the family had just bought, Ruth and a girl friend were given permission to go up there and have a look at the empty place as long as they stayed with her relatives. But the two girls decided to rough it and sleep at the other house, which had stood empty for many years.

Ruth and Marjory set up two army cots in an upstairs bedroom. There was an enclosed staircase leading to the upper floor, and a door at the bottom of it. The first night in the old house, the two girls, feeling adventurous, cooked a meal on a stove they had brought with them. They were tired and went to bed fairly early.

Falling asleep almost immediately, Ruth was awakened by the sound of someone walking up the stairs. Marjory, who also heard it, sat up straight in bed and listened. It was a bright, moonlit night and they could clearly see each other across the room. The footsteps sounded like the steps of a heavy man. When they had reached the top of the stairs where there was a landing, the girls waited for the intruder to show himself, terrified, of course, as twelve-year-olds would be.

But nobody came into their room and nobody went down the stairs again. They jumped out of bed, lit whatever lamps they had, and finally opened the door. They found no one in the house except themselves, although they searched.

Ruth's cousin Harold Marvin, a student at Oberlin, in his early twenties, was staying with Ruth's uncle at the time. The next day the two girls asked him to sleep in the house with them. He agreed, and set up a cot in the front bedroom. Needless to say, it made the two girls very happy to have a man in the house, and they outdid themselves in preparing a good dinner. Afterwards, they retired to their respective rooms, the girls upstairs, and Harold directly under them.

In the middle of the night, when everyone was asleep, the footsteps started up again. Harold heard them too, for he opened his door and called up: "Ruth, are you walking around up there?"

The girls rushed downstairs and finally told

him *why* he had been invited to share the house with them. Harold did not believe in the psychic and examined the house very carefully. But he decided to stick around with them in the old house until he could find a logical explanation for the footsteps. For ten days, the three young people became ghost hunters. Every night the steps returned and every morning the three were dumbfounded.

Finally, Ruth's parents arrived with the furniture for the house, accompanied by her brother and a little dog named Trixie. Ruth's mother entered the house first, followed by Trixie. But when the dog crossed the threshold, he stopped dead in his tracks. His hair bristling, he whimpered and cried as if begging them not to go into that house! Nothing could make him go into the house, and he shot out from under them into the open yard. Ruth's mother then proceeded into the house alone. She had been psychic on occasion, and this was one of those occasions.

"There is something here!" she declared.

Ruth's father, Roy Marvin, engineer by profession, scoffed at the idea. The dog's behavior, however, upset him.

"We've made a mistake," Mrs. Marvin said, but they had bought the house and would have to make the best of it. The men were unloading the furniture now and Mrs. Marvin went inside to direct them. The rest of the family stayed outside while she entered the house ahead of the moving men, addressing herself to the unseen guest from another age. Here and there she stopped and said a prayer for his peace of mind.

When the furniture was all in place, Mrs. Marvin came out and told her family to come on in. Everything would be all right now. Even the dog no longer bolted.

They never were able to trace the previous owners, and as the house had been empty for more than thirty years, there might have been some trespassers in addition to the legal tenants. But whatever or whoever it was that walked up those stairs, walked no more.

Premonitions, true dreams and hunches filled the years as Ruth grew up. Despite several such experiences, she never involved herself in the study of the phenomena except where they concerned her personally.

Many years after her initial experience in the state of Washington, Ruth lived at Cannes on the French Riviera, married to Paul L. A friend of hers by the name of Count Antoine S. had a small villa at Cap d' Antibes called the Villa Lilliput. He had suffered from heart trouble, and as Ruth's husband owned a hotel at the spa of Royat, famed for its salubrious cures, she suggested he go there and spend some time as their guest at the hotel.

He agreed to go there with his valet, but he had invited them for dinner that night, and would go the day after. Another friend of the Count's, Princess Ghika, and two others were also present at the Count's dinner party that evening. It was a gay evening and the Count even got Ruth's promise to visit him at Royat and play cards with him during his cure. The party broke up, and Ruth was happy in the thought that her friend would be on his way to Royat the next morning for his much-needed cure.

The following night, she awoke from sleep because of a vivid nightmare. The vision was so strong she could not shake it. She had seen a walled garden with a driveway coming out of it, and there was a hole in that wall. Outside the driveway, she had seen a car. Two men came out carrying a man, and when they came closer, she saw it was her friend the Count. He seemed very white, and Ruth had the distinct impression that he was very ill and needed help.

"Do something for him," she heard herself say. Neither the garden nor the men seemed at all familiar.

But one of them said to her: "We've done all we can. I'm his doctor."

She was crying now, and replied: "Don't put him in a car, put him in a bed!"

"That's what we're doing," the man said. We're taking him back to Villa Lilliput to put him to bed."

"But he looks as if he's dead," she heard herself say.

"He is," the man replied gravely, "but we're taking him back."

Now another person entered the dream vision, the late author Somerset Maugham, whom Ruth knew very well. She turned to him now and asked that he intercede and not allow the Count's body to be driven back like that. Maugham, in the dream, replied not to worry about it and said that the Count was "a scoundrel." That of course struck Ruth as very odd. Somerset Maugham and the Count had been very good friends and she had met the Count through the author.

With that, Ruth awakened, and her husband also woke up. She discussed her nightmare with him, and her husband calmed her, or tried to, pointing out that by now the Count was already at Royat or nearby. It was 4 A.M. and he urged her to go back to sleep. But her sleep was interrupted again, this time by the ringing of the telephone. It was the manager of their hotel in Cannes. He had received a call from Princess Ghika that Count S. had died the previous night! Apparently he had gone to have dinner at her home and had taken sick after dinner. The Princess' house was on the outskirts of Cannes.

When Ruth later described her dream to her, the Princess pointed out that the walled garden was at her home, although Ruth could not have known this, never having been there.

"What did the doctor in your dream look like?" she asked Ruth.

"He looked like the man who is just coming in the door there," Ruth pointed out. They were at the bar of the hotel.

"But that *is* the doctor," the Princess said.

"The only thing strange in my dream is that you took him back to his house in the car," Ruth contined.

Meanwhile the doctor had come up and heard her remark.

"But that's exactly what we did," he confirmed "How did you know?"

Everything happened in her dream as it had simultaneously happened miles away, except for the presence of Somerset Maugham. She could not puzzle out why he had entered her psychic vision until a few days later, she received a letter from Maugham. It was an invitation to join him for lunch.

Because she knew of the close friendship between the late Count and Maugham, Ruth tried to console him over the Count's death.

"Oh, don't worry about it," Maugham said with a twinkle in his eyes. *"He was a scoundrel."*

Suddenly Ruth realized why Maugham had appeared in her psychic dream. A strange mixture of the dead reaching out to the living to let them know of their passing, and the ability of the dead to foresee the future, is at the heart of this experience.

Mrs. Thornhill has had other encounters with the Unknown. To her, at least, the Unknown is a lot less mysterious than to the person to whom nothing of this kind ever happens.

The incident with the Count happened in May, 1946. Some time afterward Ruth married Claude Thornhill, the bandleader and composer. Thornhill died in 1965, and the following year his widow moved into an apartment in one of New York's smart East Side hotels, while at the same time retaining ownership of the house she and Thornhill had bought for their weekends in nearby New Jersey.

Her husband had never had any heart

trouble. But one night in July, 1965, he suddenly complained of chest pains as he was resting quietly in bed prior to going to sleep. By the time the doctor arrived, however, he felt better. Nevertheless, he was given an injection. A few moments later he complained of feeling very odd. A moment later he was gone.

The doctor worked over him in vain. As she picked him up to put some pillows behind him, Ruth noticed a shimmering light around his head. His hair seemed full of electricity. It was just for an instant, but when it ceased she knew he was gone for good.

Mrs. Thornhill made no immediate attempt of her own to make contact with her husband. But three days after his death, a first link was made for her from "the other side," so to speak. She felt an impulse to call Bonnie Lake, a lady she scarcely knew, who had casually met her late husband only twice during his long career. Miss Lake is a writer and actress. Soon after Mrs. Thornhill obtained her address and called her, Miss Lake came to see her.

That night they tried automatic writing, a talent Miss Lake has. There was another friend present, a lady from Texas named Cathy Nells who is somewhat psychic too. Suddenly, Bonnie Lake started to write. The first words purported to come from Mrs. Thornhill's mother. They were in her style and used a favorite phrase of hers, "Now you listen to Mary." Even the handwriting seemed like her mother's. Bonnie Lake could not have known these details, as she had not met Mrs.

Thornhill until that evening.

Next the automatist wrote four bars of music. There followed a message from Ruth's late husband. The other lady, who knew Claude Thornhill's handwriting, immediately identified it, corroborating her.

"He wants you to ask questions," the medium said.

"Are you all right?" Mrs. Thornhill asked.

Immediately the pencil in Bonnie Lake's hand began to move across the paper again.

"I'm fine and on my way, *Peedee*."

Mrs. Thornhill was visibly moved. Peedee was the nickname her husband called her in private. No one but she and her husband knew the spelling of this usual name.

One night not long after, she was alone at home in the house in New Jersey. She was expecting the local minister to call and whiled away the time at the piano. She played one of her husband's compositions, "Memory of an Island." She felt she was playing it very well, and felt rather proud of herself. "He should hear this," she thought

As if in answer to her silent thought, she heard a voice speak to her: "Yes, but watch your fingering!"

The voice originated at the other end of the piano and it sounded exactly like her husband's voice in life. Shocked, she looked down at her fingers and discovered that her fingering *was* wrong. This was two months after his death, and suddenly his presence was very strong again. The bell rang. It was the minister she had been expecting, and the spell was broken.

Mrs. Thornhill kept herself busy around the house after her husband's untimely passing. On a busy summer day that same year she was stripping wallpaper from the living room walls. She was standing on a ladder, something her husband had always forbidden her to do. A young girl from the neighborhood was with her that afternoon, helping around the house. The piano was in the living room at that time. The young girl, Kay Cameron, excused herself and went into the kitchen. Mrs. Thornhill saw her pass the piano and disappear into the kitchen. That moment she heard the piano playing *by itself*. It started softly at first, as if the music came from far away; then it began to build, and her first thought was that Kay must be at the piano. The piano was playing the "Paganini Variations of Brahms," one of the pieces her late husband frequently practiced on this very piano. It was a good piece to strengthen his technique.

Ruth Thornhill came down from the ladder to look and walked to the entrance of the dining room; at the same time Kay walked in from the kitchen with a blank look on her face.

"Were you playing the piano?" the girl asked. That instant the playing stopped.

Both women had heard the music. It was the piece he had practiced on his last day. Kay had been in the house that day on a visit. She remembered it well.

After his death, Ruth Thornhill had lent the car to the band, which continued to work under a different leader. Somehow the car papers were mislaid, and when she wanted to sell the car, she could not find them. No matter how much she searched, the papers remained lost, and she finally asked her attorney to get her a duplicate set of ownership papers.

One day she was alone in the house. It was around four in the afternoon on a fall day. It had been a tiresome day filled with problems, some of them unsolved, and she stood by the window and looked out into the sunset. Suddenly she had an impulse to go over to where she had left a Ouija board the night before. The board was considered more a toy than a serious instrument of communication, but she had one in the house and used it now and again.

"Nonsense," she thought, and tried to ignore the impulse. But the urge was stronger, and finally she reached the board and placed her hands ever so lightly upon the indicator. Instantly, there was contact!

"Go to my music" was the message spelled out. "You're tired, but before you go to sleep tonight, work on my music."

Now she had been over his arrangements thousands of times. The music was all over the place—in the basement, in the garage, and it would be quite at task to look at all of it. But the message had been very insistent and there was nothing more.

She had dinner and decided she could not do any more work that night, message or no message. She went upstairs to bed, but could not fall asleep.

"It's no use," she said to herself. She got dressed again and went down into the basement of the house, standing in the middle of the piles of music around her. She had no idea where to start. Finally, she decided the only thing she could do that night would be to look through the music that had been used the time she lent the car to the band, when she had last had the documents. It seemed like a small job, just about all she might manage that night.

She picked up the piano book from the arrangements case and took it up to the dining room. She opened it, and on the third page, there were the car papers!

"I try not to call him," Mrs. Thornhill explained to me. "I feel he has a great deal of work to do. He told me he is happy and I know we will see each other again. It would be selfish of me to harp on him."

Mrs. Thornhill's "open channel" did not operate only for her late husband. There were others who wished to let her know that their existence continued, or who took an interest in what she was doing here on the physical side of life.

Shortly after she moved into her town apartment in the winter of 1966, she went to Europe. Returning in time for the Christmas holiday, she was expecting her brother Don Marvin to come from California to spend Christmas with her. Christmas dinner was shared with Kay and the man she had married. Mrs. Thornhill felt extremely tired and rather detached that evening. She describes her condition as "floaty," and that is exactly the word for the start of mediumistic conditions. Her mind was not on the conversation that evening.

When Ruth went to bed, she fell alseep almost instantly. She was awakened by raps on the wall separating the room she slept in from the one her brother was using. Her first thought on awakening was to blame the neighbors for making the noise. She saw that it was 1 A.M. when she turned on the light. She then realized it was not a party next door, but something uncanny that was disturbing her.

"If you're trying to communicate with me," she thought, "will you rap twice?"

There came two distinct raps, followed by a flurry of signals which she tried to dismiss. Underneath, she knew very well that someone was trying to reach her. She got up and went into the pantry to put on some tea. She waited a few minutes for the tea to be strong enough.

When she left the pantry and looked across the room toward the hallway leading into the bedroom, she noticed a man standing there. Her eyesight is not very good, and she thought it was her brother Don. The figure was of his height, so she was not at all afraid, but waited for him to say something and explain his presence. Instead, the figure started to dissolve *from the top down*. There was a small mirror in back of where the man stood, and gradually the mirror became visible through his body, until the body completely disappeared.

She walked over to the spot and found herself quite alone. Moreover, the door to her brother's room was tightly closed. Inside, her brother was fast asleep; the light was out, and it was obvious he had not stirred. There was no light whatsoever in the passage, nothing that could have created the illusion of a figure.

Ruth was not sure who the caller had been—not because it was a spectral figure, but because of her poor eyesight. She could not have identified even a flesh-and-blood figure under the light conditions and at the distance across the apartment from which she had been standing. She went back to bed, puzzled. Who might the person have been? From the height of the figure, she was sure that it had not been her husband. But who was it?

The man, whose facial features she had not been able to distinguish, had dark hair and wore a dark suit of some kind. That much she had seen. Back in bed, she had trouble falling asleep again, so she read for an hour and a half. Suddenly her brother rushed into her room in great excitement.

"Were you calling me?" Ruth assured him she wasn't. What had awakened him from deep sleep was the sound of a voice saying, "Don, Ruth needs you!" and at the same time he saw a figure standing beside his bed and felt someone shake him as if to arouse him. He felt the touch at the same time that he heard the voice calling. The voice had been very much like their mother's voice. Had she thought that the previous experience had so unnerved Ruth that she needed her brother's help to calm down?

Quickly she filled him in on what had happened during the two hours just past. As she spoke of the raps, the raps returned in force. Her brother had been a complete skeptic until that night, but he too heard the raps.

Eventually he returned to his room, but neither of them found any more sleep that night. It was 7 A.M. when he came back into her room. He had just listened to a television news broadcast.

"Are you awake?" he asked, and when she nodded, he added: "Well, *I know who it was.*"

"Who was it?"

"The morning news just announced that Nick Dandolas has died." The news brought an immediate reaction from Ruth. "Nick the Greek" had been a dear and close friend of hers for many years. In retrospect she realized that the dark figure indeed looked like him. The famed gambler had been psychic himself in his time, and they had often discussed their various experiences in this field.

But there was an unseen presence that kept intruding itself on her after her husband's death. This presence at times wanted to take her over, and she fought it: she did not feel that it was a welcome presence, and it frightened her despite her knowledge of the unseen world. She felt it in the house in New Jersey and in her apartment in Manhattan, but she also knew this was neither her husband nor her mother. This was someone else.

Under the circumstances I thought it wisest to send Ruth to see Betty Ritter and to examine whatever material Betty might get about any "hangers-on." Mrs. Thornhill phoned Mrs. Ritter without telling her who she was, and after some difficulty, Mrs. Ritter agreed to see her on November 8, 1967, at her apartment on the East Side. Mrs. Thornhill found Betty charming, and the two women got along well. I had asked her to keep an exact transcript of whatever was said during her sitting.

Before she went to see Betty Ritter, Ruth Thornhill had again tried her hand at the Ouija board. Her partner was the local minister, of all people, and the message purported to come from her late husband. Discounting much of it simply because it could very well have emanated from her own unconscious, there was nevertheless an urgent request contained in it which concerned Claude Thornhill's musical estate. The late composer wanted her to contact Robert Lissauer, the publisher, whom he had known for many years, and subsequently Ruth did. Now when she arrived at Betty Ritter's apartment and had scarcely sat down, Betty insisted she had just gotten a name of some importance to her, and she wrote down *Robert L.*

"A man is standing behind you: he leans down and kisses you and says: 'This is my girl!' I see a name; it is dim—I'm sure of the CL."

Betty had no idea who Mrs. Thornhill was, nor did she know that Claude Thornhill had passed on.

The communicator continued through Betty: "What can I do? It was God's will. I love you."

Betty continued her sitting, very much relaxed now, by describing some other members of Ruth's family. Then she spoke of a man who had committed suicide ... a very large and insistent S.

She added: "I see someone who hung himself... M."

Later, Mrs. Thornhill explained that a long time before, she had a suitor, a Russian gentleman initialed S. who was possessed of a large ego. When he received no encouragement from her, he eventually shot himself. This man had indeed been "insistent." But there was also another friend first-named Michael who had committed suicide by hanging when he felt himself grown old.

Was either of the two behind the insistent presence at her New York apartment and in the country house? Ruth wondered. Anyone saying "coincidence" here would be stretching a point beyond belief: two suicides, and the exact initials named, under circumstances that exclude any foreknowledge by the medium of any circumstances surrounding her caller.

"A lovely mother stands behind you," Betty continued. "Mary ... Marie? No, Mary."

Mrs. Thornhill's mother was named Mary, but her father had called her Marie.

She then told her that she was being annoyed at night in her bedroom by "someone" pulling her covers off. Ruth nodded. It was perfectly true, and she wished she knew *who* was doing it.

Betty then described a dead person, a man who was furious at something concerning a watch. He is in a temper at something that happened to him, Betty explained, and she quoted him as complaining that someone had "knocked him down."

But to Ruth this expression made immediate sense, even though the incident had happened in the 1950s and had hardly been on her mind. The gentleman friend initialed S. whom Betty had sensed as one of two suicides trying to communicate with her had indeed been involved in an incident with a watch. The watch was Ruth's, and she had asked him to have it repaired when it stopped. When she got it back, he had taken it upon himself to have his name engraved on the back of it. This made her very angry and she broke off their friendship because of it. Someone had "knocked him down," meaning "put him down." "Put him down" would have been the expression this Russian gentleman would have used!

As Betty continued her messages, she brought Ruth assurance that her husband would watch over her and protect her. "He has just handed you a large rose—he says it's his love!"

Although many people express their love with flowers, the rose had been a constant and special symbol in the Thornhills' life. Ruth considered this symbol very characteristic of Claude.

Although I was not present at this reading, I was mentioned. Betty, of course, did not know my connection with Mrs. Thornhill, but she mentioned that she "saw" something going into a book and that a writer was involved—and here I am now.

Betty Ritter then described the house she had never visited, complete even to the stacks of manuscripts lying around. During all this, Mrs. Thornhill kept her mouth shut and her mind as much a blank as she could manage.

Suddenly she said: "Ruth ... what does Ruth

mean? It must be you, because the voice said, "Do this, Ruth!' "

Mrs. Ritter thought he meant that certain business arrangements should be made concerning the "papers."

I had asked Mrs. Thornhill to let me have the transcript of her next sitting with Betty Ritter, especially those portions that seemed to prove communication with the dead.

On November 26, Ruth returned for a second visit with Betty, without, however, having disclosed anything to her concerning herself or the results of the first sitting. Immediately upon her arrival, Betty described the presence of Mrs. Thornhill's family "in spirit": "A mother ... Marie ... Charles ... William ... John, and two others ... they are a family."

Mrs. Thornhill's mother, Mary or Marie, did have seven brothers, among them John, William and Charles.

"A man standing behind you places his hands on your shoulder, smiles and says, 'This is my wife,' " Betty continued, and added that her late husband showed her that she was writing her *memoirs*—Betty had trouble with that word—and also spoke of a Dr. R., with the first initial A. The interesting thing about this message was that Dr. A. R. was a dear friend of both Ruth and Claude Thornhill; the latter had once saved his life. The doctor's wife had been urging her to write her memoirs, and she was about to do so!

"Your husband is kissing you. He is so sorry and seems to repent about something. He shows me the words 'exchange' and 'stock market,' things dwindling down ... I see him on his knees beside you."

Apparently Mr. Thornhill had bought some stocks against his wife's advice, and had refused to sell them when she suggested that he do so. They were now quite worthless. As there were not many of them, the matter was not very important to Ruth, but her husband would have taken precisely the attitude Betty described—exaggerating where his wife's welfare was concerned.

To further prove his identity—not that Ruth doubted it by now—Betty Ritter described her husband bringing in a woman now whom he called Louise. The interesting fact is that Mr. Thornhill had always carried a small card with Aunt Louise's name on it, a card which Louise's husband, her uncle, had given him after her death. Mr. Thornhill was quite sentimental about it and about her.

But the door to the Other Side allowed others to pass through to greet her, too. Evidently her own psychic potential had been added in some way to Betty's for an overall topnotch reading.

"I see the spirit of a man with mustache, hard of hearing in his left ear. He had to do with chemicals. Peter ... and he said, show you the anchor of a ship."

Such a detailed and specific message would certainly be capable of verification, I thought, when Mrs. Thornhill showed me the transcript. Needless to say, Betty still knew nothing whatever about Ruth or her friends.

Well, some years ago Mrs. Thornhill had befriended a gentleman named Peter. He had a mustache, was hard of hearing in one ear, and was an executive with Shell Oil, in charge of some tankers. It had been many years since she saw him, and a check in the London telephone directory showed only his wife—or widow—listed...

Not every person is as fortunate as Ruth Thornhill in making contact with the Beyond both personally and through an intermediary. Perhaps she is a better channel than most, and, having served others as psychic spokeswoman, she was rewarded by meeting the right people to allow her an evidential contact through a medium like Betty Ritter.

The material Ruth has obtained in her two sessions with Betty, reinforced by her own primary experiences with the surviving personalities of her husband and several others whom she knew, has given her the conviction that life does indeed continue and we need not fear death or consider a separation caused by the dissolution of the physical body as final.

In telling her personal story, I hope I'm reaching out to the many who have wondered about such things and who may have had similar proof themselves but have not been sure.

# HOW TO OVERCOME NEGATIVITY

## *(Psycho-Ecstasy)*

Essentially humankind is divided into three great groups as far as attitude towards life is concerned. There are those who see everything optimistically, the pollyannas of this world who refuse to acknowledge the existence of evil or bad influences and who will only see that which is good and positive. Then there are those who are born pessimists, who emphasize the negative in life and have little use for the optimist. To the pessimist, anything positive happening or about to happen is nearly one step from disappointment. Whenever the pessimist cannot explain some positive situation away entirely, he or she will minimize its impact by pointing out that most of that which occurs in this world of ours is negative and destructive. Between these two extremes there is the vast majority of people who accept both positive and negative values as natural and as part of the eternal challenge of life. That, of course, is the only healthy attitude. If everything happening to us were entirely positive and without flaw, then there would be no effort required to cope with it.

There would be no challenge, no testing of a person's character and mettle. On the other hand, if all were negative, there would be no hope, no encouragement to try, and that too would be an impossible world.

It must be clearly understood in the context of this work that I do not propose to ignore existing conditions simply because they do not contribute to progress. Negative situations are as valid as positive situations; in fact, sometimes the negative produces greater results than the positive. For example, the continuing warfare in Europe has produced a sharper, more sophisticated culture in general than the culture in some parts of the world which were never touched by warfare, destruction, and suffering. No one can deny that Great Britain and Germany and France, three of the main warfaring countries during the last few centuries, have contributed to many aspects of progress both on the technical and the cultural level. On the other hand, little Switzerland, which has not seen any warfare since the Middle Ages, has found its purpose and fulfillment as a nation in other directions. Adversity is always a character builder, although not necessarily a desirable one. There is another way. Suffering is not a necessity. Feelings of guilt are worthless and human-created. Actions, whether on the physical level or on the mental-emotional-thought level, are all that counts. Since nations are only the sum total of large numbers of individuals and the institutions created and maintained by them, the solution must be found within the individual. How, then, can the average individual overcome negative conditions?

A negative condition can be one of two things: it is either the absence of something positive, useful, desired, necessary, or it is the faulty state of something that is essentially positive. By its own definition a negative condition is undesirable, with the sole exception, already noted, that it can sometimes contribute to a strengthening of character in the individual. That, however, is a temporary state of affairs, and prolonged negative conditions do not contribute to character improvement but will inevitably lead to destruction.

The first step to overcome negative conditions is to recognize them. This is not as obvious as it may sound. Many individuals are not even aware of the fact that something in their lives is negative or destructive. For example, take the case of Mr. K.—in good health, in his middle fifties, well educated, and a family man. He has held one position practically all his adult life. He has acquired certain skills even though they are not outstanding. He works in an industry in which there is keen competition for jobs. Nevertheless, his record is fine and he is generally recognized as a man of quality and integrity. Despite this, he has advanced very little in thirty years on the same job. He is too polite to ask for an advancement and too filled with fears of losing his job to try to look elsewhere. In fact, he is so worried that one might hear of his potential interest in a position somewhere else that he has refused to have lunch with anyone working for a competitive company. Does Mr. K. think that his attitude is negative? Not at all. He is firmly convinced that he is prudent and very well off. His wife does not think so. She wants him to try and better himself, to look elsewhere or to make new contacts in his own company, to find a better position for himself after such prolonged and faithful service. But Mr. K. cannot do this because he doesn't agree with his wife's view. What to her seems like a self-imposed form of slavery, a total lack of progress and therefore a negative condition, is to her husband merely a proper satisfactory attitude. Unless Mr. K. recognizes the negative connotation of his position and his relationship to those he works for, he will not be able to do anything about it.

Miss W. is in her middle twenties, works as a secretary in a large eastern city, and is deeply in love with her boss. Her boss, twenty years her senior, is happily married and has given her no reason to hope for a divorce. Nevertheless, Miss W. continues her relationship with her boss even though an outsider, if familiar with the situation, would readily see that it had no future whatsoever. But Miss W. does not want to see her situation in such a light. She does not realize that her relationship with her boss has strong negative aspects. Thus she is unable to leave him and find a better relationship elsewhere. It is impossible for her to change her negative situation, simply because she doesn't recognize it as such.

Mr. F. has suffered from migraine headaches for twenty years. He works in a factory in the state of Pennsylvania and spends most of his working hours in confined, damp, and very noisy quarters.

He is fully aware of the fact that his working conditions are less than desirable and has frequently expressed a dislike for his job, but he has never done anything about a change and has continued to stay with the same company. As the years went by, a nagging headache started to develop. When he consulted one doctor after another, he found that no organic cause for his headache could be detected. Eventually he sought out a psychiatrist who subjected him to the usual tests. When the psychiatrist discovered the conflict between the man's desire to change jobs and his inability to do anything about it, he quickly realized that the migraines were caused by this inner conflict. He explained the situation to Mr. F. Unfortunately, Mr. F. did not understand or decided not to accept the theories of psychoanalysis and rejected this explanation as farfetched. He still has his headaches and tries to find an organic cause for them. Although he would like to make a change in his working conditions, he cannot possibly understand how such a problem could in any way influence his nervous system. Thus Mr. F. does not recognize the negative situation in his life either and cannot do anything about it.

Let us assume, however, that the individual who wants to overcome negative conditions in his or her life does understand them and recognize them as such. The first thing to do is to see if they can be physically altered. If a position is unsatisfactory, one must try and find a better one. If a state of health gives one cause for concern, one must consult with appropriate authorities. If a romantic attachment is a dead-end situation, one must break it off and seek greener pastures. These are obvious directions in which to go and need not be further explained. However, if such direct action is impossible, the individual need not necessarily accept the continuing negative situation as inevitable and hopeless. If the situation itself cannot be changed, then one's attitude towards it must be altered. This concept is based upon a startling fact: nothing in this world of ours has reality until and unless we become aware of it and relate to it either by our senses or through thoughts. In relating to a person or situation or even an object, our personal attitude is also involved. We relate to a person and either like or dislike him or her. We relate to a situation by either enjoying it or not enjoying it. We relate to an object by either appreciating it or not appreciating it. In each case, whether it is a relationship between one individual or another individual, situation, or object, there is a personal involvement brought into play as well. Personal involvement means attitude, opinion, view, feelings, thoughts, and reactions. What happens within us is of prime importance to the ensuing result. Our reactions and feelings are much closer to our inner selves than the subject or object of our attention.

Let us take the same three people who have not seen the negative aspects of their situations and assume that they do see the situations as they are in reality. What can they do about them? Mr. K. will suddenly realize the negative aspects of his situation and decide he doesn't like it. However, until such time as he is able to take positive action to alter it, he will accept it as a temporary situation. The first step to overcoming negative situations is to accept them temporarily and to do something about changing them. Meantime, Mr. K. is not going to go into his office in the morning and tell his boss off or tear the papers on his desk and walk out, ego triumphant. He will, however, use all his spare time to make new contacts or improve relations with his own superiors while at the same time performing his duties as well as ever. From that moment on, when his decision has been made to try and alter his conditions, the negative aspects of his current situation will seem less frustrating. As a matter of fact, there will be a certain gusto with which he now applies himself to the job he really hates. He wants to leave in a blaze of glory. As a result, one of two things will happen. Either he will find a more satisfactory position and change jobs, or his sudden zest in a position he has held for thirty years will come to the attention of his superiors and they, in turn, might work Mr. K. into a more satisfactory slot. Either way he gains. Has anything actually changed? Only Mr. K.'s attitude has.

What about Miss W. and her love for her boss? She recognizes the uselessness of her relationship and mentally frees herself from the ties which have thus far prevented her striking out elsewhere. Suddenly she looks at other men with new eyes. She looks at herself in a different way — not as an attractive woman, but as a free individual capable of attracting someone new and exciting. As a result of this newly found courage, she projects precisely that and before long finds a new and more satisfactory relationship. Has anything changed? Has she changed her makeup, her clothes, her hairdo? Not necessarily. The only thing she has changed is her attitude towards a negative situation. All that time she maintained her friendship with her boss. But there is a difference: she is no longer emotionally dependent upon him. Again, there are two possibilities: she will free herself from his influence the moment someone new appears on the scene, or her less dependent attitude towards her boss and lover spurs his emotions to a point where he must make a decision. If he loves her as much as she loves him, perhaps there will be a divorce and the two might yet get together. Either way, Miss W.'s changed attitude can only result in gains for her.

Mr. F. would also look differently at his migraine headaches if he recognized the connection between his sufferings and his frustrations. In his case the results would be even more dramatic. Immediately upon his realizing the connection between headaches and job frustration, and the firm resolution to do something about it the next morning, the headaches will disappear. Of course, if Mr. F. fails to put into action what he has decided, they will recur, but so long as he is actively engaged in altering his situation he will not suffer from migraine headaches any longer.

But in addition to recognizing when negative conditions exist and changing one's attitude towards them, there are two other elements necessary to accomplish the desired results. The third factor involves a proper evaluation of the reasons why negative conditions exist. Most people who are not familiar with my techniques will blame themselves, bad luck, lack of talent or ability, a vengeful God, jealousy, or simply situations beyond their control for the existence of negative conditions in their lives. They will look at them totally negatively in that they see no good whatsoever in such conditions. But every negative condition already contains, within itself, the germ of future positive resolution. The advanced individual will look at these negative situations, and though he may not know what lies ahead in the way of overcoming them, he will somehow feel that they may not have come his way or that he would not have been subjected to these conditions unless they were meant to teach him something. In overcoming, we always learn. Later, in retrospect, we inevitably realize how valuable the negative situation has been in the long pull, even though at the time it happens to us it is totally undesirable and rejected by us. But fate cannot fill a vacancy until one exists. A room filled with air cannot be filled with more air—a vacuum, however, can and will be. To create such a vacuum in our lives is the purpose of negative conditions. Without them, positive conditions cannot take their place.

Mr. A. is a successful attorney in the city of New York. He held a good position with a law firm for several years. Suddenly he was dismissed from his job. He blamed office politics, not understanding the reasons for his dismissal. A week later he met an old friend whom he had not seen for several years. Over lunch Mr. A. was made a proposition involving much travel. It was an exciting and new assignment which he could only accept if he were free to travel. If A. had still been on his job he would have surely rejected this proposition, since he considered his position secure and desirable. Now, however, without a job, he readily accepted and found the new assignment very much more to his liking than the old one had been. If fate had not arranged for him to lose his position and thus create a negative situation, A. would not have been ready to accept the step forward in his career.

The best way to look at negative situations, whether they are in the field of work, personal emotional involvement, health, or otherwise, is to try and eliminate all panic, all irrational attitudes, and to detach oneself as much as possible from the situation as if it were happening to someone else. Calmly looking into the reasons or seeming reasons for the situation to exist, one will then find that despite the essentially negative aspects of it there are already some possible developments included in it and that these positive developments might yet undo the damage done by the negative situation. I am not saying that one should minimize the seriousness of any existing situation, but seriousness is not the same as hopelessness. There is always, or nearly always, a way to cope with undesirable conditions. *There are no bad breaks. There are only good breaks in disguise.* Mr. A.'s being fired was, on the surface at least, a bad break.

Finding a better position the following week was certainly a good break. Thus the bad break was really a good break in disguise. And so it goes in many areas of life and with the majority of people, if they will only recognize conditions from that point of view.

A fourth factor to be considered when coping with negative conditions is even more important than the first three. Having recognized the existence of a negative situation and changed one's attitude towards it and finally tried to analyze the reasons why such a situation had come about in one's particular case, there still remains the need to apply a positive, outgoing factor, before positive results can be obtained. This is the technique of creating a wish-fulfillment thought in one's own mind and projecting it outward into the world, both at home and when having contact with people in one's field of work or in the area in which one's negative situation lies. The result is sometimes startling.

Mr. J. S. was an assistant producer of a Hollywood daytime serial popularly known as a soap opera. Suddenly he was dismissed from his job. He blamed personal jealousy instead of economics. Had he not been trained in this method of projecting a thought-fulfillment image, he would have been despondent and would have aired his frustrations to anyone willing to listen. Instead, he shrugged and immediately started to build himself a better, more desirable career. He had long wanted to have a leading production job in one of the most important nighttime serials in television.

Now he started to project himself as such a person, sending forth the image of himself in the new, desired position, when he was alone as well as when he made the rounds of the offices within his industry. Within a matter of weeks he had made the right contacts and his name was proposed for the position of second in command on that very nighttime program he had wanted to work on. He is now the associate producer of it and far happier than he ever was in his previous position.

A skeptic might say that these four steps, interesting though they are, will not make a broken leg whole or cure an incurable physical affliction. The skeptic is wrong, even though these four steps in overcoming negative conditions are primarily on the personality level of the individual and deal with physical conditions only in a secondary and indirect way. There are, in addition to the four steps, invisible but very tangible psychic forces set in motion by their application that can and will alter the process of healing. It is a medical fact that a positive attitude and expectancy towards healing will make a patient get well that much faster. Projecting a positive force never hurts and can only bring positive results. No matter what, the one who applies this technique will be no worse off than he would be if he did not know of it. Very likely, he will be much better off if he applies it correctly. The results may well be startling.

# MEDICAL MEN AND UNORTHODOX HEALING

## *(Beyond Medicine)*

Even though the august American Society for Psychical Research has maintained a medical section for many years, and even though individual doctors have expressed an interest in psychical research and ESP, the society and these individual doctors did this apart from the medical profession, carefully avoiding any clash with the American Medical Association. To the majority of physicians, the idea that a healer without a degree in medicine could accomplish part or all of what the medical doctor is trained to do is not only unthinkable but downright in conflict with his or her own best interests as a professional.

There are exceptions, of course. Enlightened physicians have learned, if nothing else, that their knowledge is limited. Such physicians welcome information and new facts from any source, whether or not that source has been given the official stamp of approval through the bestowal of a medical degree.

Doctors who admit the existence of unorthodox healing are usually quick to explain that we do not know why and how such cures come about. Even though they readily admit the existence of healing outside of orthodox medicine, they are far from recognizing the purveyors of such healing practices as their equals or even as professionals. The only difference between the skeptical doctor and the enlightened one, in this respect, is in the nomenclature: the orthodox physician calls anyone not an orthodox physician a quack; the enlightened doctor, who admits the possibility that healing works, refers to healers as lay healers or untrained healers. It does not occur to him or her that the training that the unorthodox healer has had or the knowledge that he or she has obtained one way or another also constitutes a body of learning, although different from conventional education.

On the other hand, there are a few courageous medical doctors who not only acknowledge the existence of unorthodox healing, including psychic healing, as a reality, but who go so far as to include it in their own work if they are fortunate enough to have psychic healing powers in their makeup to the extent that they can be called upon in their medical work. Naturally such M.D.'s would be subject to persecution by their own fraternity as well as by various government agencies if they were to admit to this activity openly and freely. We have not yet reached the point in our society where one can dispense medical assistance outside officially approved channels.

It stands to reason that there would be a certain percentage of the psychically gifted among professional doctors as well as among other segments of the population. Some of these gifted individuals may use their extrasensory powers without realizing that they possess them: the physician whose diagnosis is nearly always correct, the doctor who puts his or her hands on a patient without administering any medicine and finds that the patient responds immediately. Such matters are frequently dismissed as "excellent bedside manners," "psychological effects," or, at the very best, intuition.

Even the term intuition is suspect in the eyes of the orthodox physician; for it implies the coming into play of feelings, something the old-fashioned practitioner of the medical arts despises. Emotional reactions and textbook medicine are deadly enemies. But unless more and more medical doctors with impeccable records as physicians come forward and freely admit that they have used or are using their psychic healing powers to help their patients, and study these effects, and publish them so that the skeptical element among their colleagues might benefit from this knowledge, psychic healing and other forms of unorthodox medicine are likely to remain scorned by the very individuals who could apply these methods better than anyone.

Not all medical doctors refuse to be identified with some form of research in this area, however. Several years ago I was invited to participate in a forum discussion on psychotherapy. The meeting was under the sponsorship of the Parapsychology Foundation and the late Eileen Garrett. To my surprise, one of the participants was an old acquaintance whom I had not seen in many years, Dr. Walter Engel, the noted psychoanalyst and pupil of Carl Jung. Dr. Engel explained that he had lately become very much interested in psychical research and was no longer hostile to the idea that humans might possess extraordinary powers, which a trained researcher could tap and use with favorable results.

Another psychoanalyst of great stature, Dr. Robert Laidlaw, for years worked with Eileen Garrett and, after her death, continued his interest in parapsychology, including psychic healing. In fact, it was he and a group of others who lately investigated the English healer George Chapman. While this does not necessarily constitute blanket approval of all healers or all healing practices, it does constitute a step forward in that these eminent medical professionals are seriously investigating the powers of individual healers. They are not doing so for their own amusement or to gratify their curiosity. They are doing this in order to learn more about the art of healing

At the University of California, Los Angeles, Dr. Thelma Moss had been investigating psychic healing with a group of associates. Their investigation includes laboratory experiments in which a healer is brought together with actual patients. The results are carefully observed and recorded. Dr. Wilhelm Beyer, a general practitioner of Überlingen, Germany, has been interested in healing approaches to possession and obsession for many years.

Another European doctor, the psychiatrist L. Kling of Strasbourg, France, has for some time specialized in the treatment of the so-called "possessed" with the well-known parapsychologist Professor G. Frei. Dr. Kling had looked into the possibility that some of the schizophrenic cases he had been dealing with might be cases of possession and therefore accessible to treatment by other methods than the conventional ones. In 1967 he sent me one of his patients, J. P. Kieffer, who had been judged a schizophrenic. "Psychiatrically speaking the diagnosis is clear, but that isn't enough by any means," Dr. Kling wrote. He explained that the subject was rational most of the time and understood fully what implications were involved. I met the man in Paris and questioned him thoroughly. My findings indicated that the individual was indeed mediumistic and subject to influences from discarnates.

Dr. Edward Bach, of London, England, was probably the greatest pioneer of herbal medicine. Originally trained as a conventional physician and bacteriologist, Dr. Bach soon broke away from his early teachings and set out to discover the healing powers of plants. "His ideal of a simple way to heal all disease persisted, and as he grew older it became a conviction and the activating force behind his whole life's work," writes Dr. Bach's biographer, Nora Weeks, in *The Medical Discoveries of Edward Bach, Physician.* "For throughout the years he practiced as pathologist, bacteriologist, and homeopath, his one aim was to find pure remedies, a simple form of treatment to replace the complicated scientific means which gave no certainty of cure. As a homeopathic physician, Dr. Bach followed the dictum to treat the patient and not the disease—that is to say, to treat the characteristics and the personality of the patient as well as the illness itself. Dealing with a part of the body apart from the whole, as is the custom in conventional medicine, is contrary to the beliefs held by homeopathic physicians. Bach's books, notably *The Twelve Healers and Other Remedies* and *Heal Thyself,* which is called an explanation of the real cause and cure of disease, are still available, and a newsletter dealing with Bach's amazing herbal treatments can be obtained from the Dr. Edward Bach Healing Centre, Mount Vernon, Sotwell, Wallingford, Berkshire, England.

Dr. J. Z. is a young physician affiliated with a Long Island, New York, hospital. "Since my third year in medical school," the doctor explained, cautiously, "I have often *felt* diagnoses before they were confirmed by clinical and laboratory testing. I am not saying that these were intuitive feelings, but rather a sort of 'sixth sense' about what the patient had. I am sure that these feelings had a lot to do with my medical knowledge combined with common sense, but these feelings went beyond this realm. I have often diagnosed and been correct despite what the medical signs had indicated. These diagnoses could not be simply explained. They were in the realm of a feeling that came to me. I am not saying that I am some sort of physician mystic, diagnosing by an inner voice. I have not uncommonly been wrong. These feelings, however, have been borne out a good percentage of times than I feel would be coincidental. I am not advocating practicing medicine or diagnosing on the basis of these feelings. I am simply saying that these feelings have occurred, exist, and will probably continue to happen."

Dr. H. W. is the principal psychiatrist at a major correctional institution in the eastern United States. He also has a private practice in psychiatry and is a respected physician. Dr. W. and I together have attempted various experiments with healing.

Even though he seeks no patients, having more than enough to do as it is, I have on occasion sent him cases from among those who appeal to me for help. In some cases Dr. W. has paid personal visits; in others he has arranged for absent healing, that is to say, telepathic sending forth of energies channeled to the particular needs of the patient. Dr. W. has never guaranteed any results when unorthodox means were employed, nor does he feel that a healer should ever do so.

Dr. W., a member of his county's medical association, has been affiliated with several large state hospitals and a private psychiatric hospital prior to the state hospital for criminals with which he is now connected. He has practiced medicine for about thirty years, primarily as a psychiatrist although he was in general practice for the first ten years of his medical career, and his comments made during an interview on medicine, psychic healing, and related subjects are very significant.

"Do you know of any cases where psychic healing has entered the picture successfully?" I asked him in the interview.

"Yes."

"Have you yourself ever witnessed any cases of psychic healing?"

"I've not only witnessed them, I've *done* them," he said.

"What were the diseases involved? Were those mental or physical diseases?"

"To my knowledge I have only been able to help mental diseases."

"For instance?"

"I have a very busy psychiatric practice," Dr. W. went on. "I found that I was mentally healing some of my patients without touching them or going near them. This realization came very gradually. I found that I was putting *too much of myself* into my patients."

"Do you mean to say that you've had actual success healing patients without the ordinary methods of interview and analysis?"

"I felt that there was a psychic thing happening, that I actually helped the patient with the nonverbal part of my mind. *I felt that I was actually pushing energy at them to heal them.*"

"Did you see this energy pass?" I asked.

"No."

"Did you feel anything going from you to the patient?"

"Yes. It felt like I was pushing an invisible beam of energy toward them."

"Did you put any specific thoughts onto that beam or was it just a general power?"

"Just a general force," he said. "I'm sure that this force exists."

"Did some of your patients ever comment upon being healed in this manner?"

"No."

"Did you ever ask them about it?"

"No."

"Have you ever considered yourself psychic?"

"Yes."

"Have you had ESP experiences?"

"Yes. I can predict the death of a patient within an hour. I did this repeatedly in a hospital; I said that a particular patient was going to die within a particular hour of a particular night."

"What made you foretell these things?"

"It just came into my mind spontaneously along with the particular patient."

"Did you ever diagnose patients by unusual means?"

"No more unusual than any other *good* internist or psychiatrist. They all do it, but may not be aware of it."

"Have you ever seen the human aura?"

"No."

"Do you accept its existence?"

"Yes."

"What do you think it is?"

"The biomagnetic field of the human being."

"When you send out a force, does it connect with the physical body of the patient or with this bioelectrical field?"

"The biomagnetic field. There are *two* of them in every human being, and they are detectable by instruments; this has been known since 1936. They are the alpha and beta fields."

"Can you tell me some incidents in your medical career where seemingly miraculous healing or spontaneous healing has taken place due to your agency?"

"I've done more with my hands placed close to their head than I have been able to do across a room."

"Have you actually cured a case where orthodox methods have failed?"

"I had one girl just recently who was very hysterical in a sudden attack provoked by fear. I straightened her out in two minutes flat."

"How did you do that?"

"With my hands."

"How did you use your hands?"

"In her particular case I used one hand a couple of inches in front of the head and the other behind."

"Do you stay still or do you move the hands about?"

"I don't move them."

"How long do you stay in that position?"

"A minute or two. That's about all it takes."

"Does the patient feel anything while that goes on?"

"Heat."

"Is this healing permanent? In this specific case you're referring to, did she then have no further recurrence of the problem?"

"Not as far as I know. They would have called me."

"In your stay at the state hospital where, I believe, you were a resident psychiatrist for a number of years, have you ever tried healing on some of the inmates?"

"Mentally, yes. On one occasion five of us took a man over a shock. He had been told in error that he could go home; we had to take him into a room and tell him that he couldn't."

"Who were the others?"

"Correction officer, supervisor, and two professional employees."

"How did he react?"

"He did not go into the violence we had expected, nor did he become depressed or suicidal as we had feared."

"Was this perhaps due to logical thinking and talking rather than any form of healing?"

"No."

"Do you think healing took place?"

"Yes."

"In which way?"

"Simply by the mental force of the five individuals involved."

Dr. W. makes no extraordinary claims as far as his healing powers are concerned, but the fact that he combines orthodox knowledge of psychiatry with a natural gift for healing is in itself remarkable. One must keep in mind, of course, that psychiatry itself deals with mental forces and that therefore the relationship between psychiatry and psychic healing would naturally be a close one if properly understood and applied. But healing has been used successfully in the more physical branches of medicine as well.

One of the most extraordinary medical personalities of our time is Dr. Douglas Baker, a native of London who has spent his growing years in Natal, South Africa. Dr. Baker was slated to take a leading place in commerce and to become the managing director of a large printing concern. Despite his assured position in commerce, he had taken an early interest in the study of zoology and of aboriginal languages and communication. At the University of Natal he became interested in the mysteries of the Zulus, and in studying their strange means of communication became aware of telepathy for the first time. He graduated with a Bachelor of Arts degree in 1949, but his interest in the world of the occult persisted, eventually forcing him to enter a retreat to think things out for himself. As a result of this mystical and spiritual experience he decided to change his life and began the study of medicine so that he could devote himself to helping humankind.

At the age of thirty-five he entered medical school in England. He qualified in medicine in 1964. He edited the medical society journal, *North Wing*, and while researching the history of medicine became interested in magnetism as a possible therapeutic agent. With George De La Warr, who had developed a radionic instrument that would prove to be useful in what Dr. Baker came to call biomagnetism, he delved into various mysteries of human personality, including the photographing of thought forms as well as the study of magnetism in relation to human personality and the body. As a result of their research in 1967 Dr. Baker and George De La Warr published *Biomagnetism — Preliminary Studies of the Effect of Magnetic Fields on Living Tissues and Organs in the Human Body*, a highly technical book describing the techniques the two men had developed and their applications and possible results from these applications. The same team followed up the first book with *Double Blind Clinical Trials to Assess the Effect of Electromagnetism on Serum Cholesterol, Prothrombin Time and Blood Pressure,* and a large teaching hospital in London, St. Mary's, investigated some of their findings, undertaking clinical trials using the equipment developed by that company. Subsequently a paper was published confirming that magnetism appears to affect the blood pressure, the level of blood cholesterol, and the clotting time of blood.

In essence the magnetic therapy units used by Dr. Douglas Baker consist of a console containing a tape recorder with tapes specially programmed for various diseases. These tapes in turn activate the creation of a low-level electromagnetic field, which is transferred to various points of the human body through solenoids placed directly on selected spots of the body where, in the opinion of Dr. Baker, the magnetic energy should be applied for best results. (Purely experimentally Dr. Baker has also developed a larger unit fitting around the head and another fitting around an arm or wrist.)

A low-level magnetic field is set up and maintained for anywhere between five and thirty minutes. The treatments are no miracle cures, and frequent application is necessary to obtain results. Dr. Baker's treatment presently works best with the lowering of blood cholesterol and blood pressure, important factors in coronary diseases and in the treatment of postcoronary cases. He has also been able to obtain significant lowering of blood sedimentation rates in arthritic complaints. Less spectacular but no less important are beneficial results obtained with this treatment in cases of eczema, shingles, and general hypertension.

Patients feel absolutely nothing, nor are there any side effects from the treatment. Patients can take the treatment at Dr. Baker's country clinic or in London. Dr. Baker has developed ambulatory units, as well, and in certain cases the patient may use a home unit.

I first met Dr. Douglas Baker at his country house at Little Elephant, Kentish Lane, Essenden, Herefordshire, England, in the summer of 1970. He showed my wife and me around the premises, including the laboratory and the cubicles upstairs used for the treatment of his patients, and we discussed his methods. Later he arranged to send me one of his units, which I've had in my possession ever since.

The presence of Dr. Baker's unit in my office has brought some fringe benefits to the cause of biomagnetism that were not originally expected of it. When Shawn Robbins, a young psychic I have trained and worked with for some time, asked that

I attempt to help her with her somewhat restricted eyesight and headaches, I suggested that she try the biomagnetic healing method.

The machine in my office is there purely for experimental purposes, and no treatments are administered to outsiders. However, in the use of Dr. Baker's machine on Shawn Robbins and other psychics I have worked with, such as John Gaudry, a remarkable development was observed: their psychic perception increased by as much as 100 percent. Not only did the magnetic field set up by the machine clear whatever complaints the mediums came to me with, such as headaches or eye strain, but their psychic abilities were remarkably stronger immediately after the treatments.

One can only conclude that the magnetic field in some way joined with the natural magnetic field within the personality of the mediums to create a stronger psychic force. We do not as yet know a great deal about the manner in which psychic ability is focused and applied, so there remains much to be researched in this area. However, Dr. Baker's biomagnetic apparatus has definitely been tied to significant changes in the performance rate of several psychics tested by me over long periods of time.

Dr. Douglas Baker's research is clearly significant, as is indicated by the reaction to his 1970 U.S. speaking tour, arranged by Dr. Robert Laidlaw, the well-known psychiatrist and head of the department of psychiatry at Roosevelt Hospital, New York.

During his many lectures Dr. Baker made no

extravagant claims. With his British sense of understatement he merely presented what he had found to be factual.

"It is natural that there are problems to be overcome in presenting a new discovery which is outside current medical orthodoxy," Dr. Baker says. "The caution with which the medical profession treats any new departures is absolutely proper. At the same time caution must not lead to apathy or make impossible the impartial scrutiny of a potentially beneficial discovery. Caution has been a prime concern of Magnetic Research, Ltd., lest anything should leak out which might stimulate unfounded hopes on the part of sufferers from certain serious diseases. The company has not indulged in so-called fringe medicine; nor does it claim to cure—though in fact its case books contain many incidents of difficult conditions alleviated through applications of magnetism. What it does claim is to have discovered a technique of applying magnetic fields with the assistance of medical knowledge in such a way that changes are recorded in subsequent laboratory tests. Thus the company has accumulated clinical evidence that by the methods it has developed new therapeutic approaches may be possible to certain diseases which until now have proved intractable to orthodox medicine."

Between five and ten thousand people have consulted Dr. Baker and been treated by his methods. *Psychic News* quotes the wife of a medical doctor who had suffered for years with a disease called purpura. The doctor's wife is quoted as stating,

"My husband gave me up and was delighted that I had found an unorthodox treatment which helped my complaint." Another patient, a teenage boy suffering from extremely low blood cholesterol causing frequent blackouts, is quoted as stating that the doctor's weak pulsating magnetic field treatment had raised his blood cholesterol to a normal level. When the treatment was stopped the young man's blood cholesterol reverted to its abnormally low level again.

According to the same source, a middle-aged man with high blood pressure and an arthritic knee testified to general improvement after a session with Dr. Baker's magnetic instrument.

Before the treatment he could hardly walk and had had to change his job to avoid exercise. After the treatment he returned to his original overseer's work, his blood pressure greatly reduced.

One would think that a man with the proper medical credentials who turns out to be a pioneer in progressive medicine, trying to expand the horizons of knowledge by as yet unorthodox but apparently valid methods, would be welcomed by the medical fraternity and officialdom as well. Yet in California, during a talk on "Magnetism, Its History and Current Applications" in which Dr. Baker outlined some of the discovered effects of magnetism and radionics, mentioned in his 1967 book, *Biomagnetism*, claimed that magnetism had affected the blood pressure of his subjects—specifically mentioning Reverend the Honorable Andrew Elphinstone—and described how some twenty out of thirty rheumatoid arthritics had responded favorably to magnetic treatment, two plainclothes detectives from the Los Angeles Police Department taped his talk and then arrested him. It was alleged that these were false claims and that, in fact, any suggestion that magnetism or radionics are healing and treating methods is false. Dr. Baker's radionics and magnetic instruments were confiscated.

Fortunately Dr. Baker was able to obtain the help of a prominent authority specializing in medical jurisprudence, Mark Joseff, Ph.D., who secured Dr. Baker's immediate release and, subsequently, a reduction of the charges.

When news of the incredible charges against Dr. Douglas Baker, a member of the College of Surgeons, was released, researchers all around the world rallied to his cause, and in September, 1971, all charges against Dr. Baker were totally dismissed—leaving only a sizable debt incurred in the defense of Dr. Baker, not to mention the unnecessary cost to the taxpayer. Why would the Los Angeles District Attorney choose to attack a man of Dr. Baker's standing? Could it be that some of his colleagues in the AMA felt threatened by the possibilities of new methods, methods that seem to be promising in the treatment of disease, and methods with which they themselves were not familiar since their own education lay back some years?

The late Dr. Herman P. Saussele, was born in Germany. He came to the United States at age fourteen and worked at first in the family bakery business in St. Louis. But all through his life he was interested in the esoteric and wanted to dedicate himself to the art of healing. Finally, at age fifty-eight, he entered the Missouri Chiropractic College and completed its four-year course, graduating as a practicing doctor of chiropractic in St. Louis. Before his recent death at eighty-five, *Healthways* magazine, the magazine of the American Chiropractic Association, reported, "Dr. Saussele is an unusual individual, a bouncing man in his mid-seventies who boasts, 'I haven't been sick since 1929 and that is quite a statement to make in 1968.'"

I met Dr. Saussele in St. Louis a few years ago. In a modest suite at 3189 South Grand Boulevard, Dr. Saussele dispensed a combination of nutritional counsel, general psychological advice on the art of proper living, chiropractic when and where needed or requested, and a fascinating field of unorthodox medicine called *iridology*.

Dr. Saussele follows the teachings of a pioneer in the field of iridology, another chiropractor by the name of Dr. Bernard Jensen, whose book, *The Science and Practice of Iridology*, published in 1952 at Hidden Valley Health Ranch, Escondido, California, is a kind of bible for the few practitioners of this very special form of healing. "By way of definition," Dr. Jensen writes, "iridology is a science whereby the doctor or operator can tell from the markings or signs in the iris of the eye the reflex condition of the various organs of the body. In other words, it is the science of determining acute, sub-acute, chronic, and destructive stages in the affected organs of the body through their corresponding areas in the iris. Drug deposits, inherent weaknesses, and living habits of the patient are also revealed in the iris of the eye."

According to this method tissue changes resulting from proper or improper treatment also show up in the iris of the patient. Thus it is possible to determine whether a prescription or treatment actually works through periodical checkup and iris diagnosis. Dr. Jensen points out the comparatively low percentage of accurate diagnoses obtained by conventional medical methods and offers the iris diagnoses as an addition to the storehouse of medical knowledge, not to replace any existing methods. And as Dr. Jensen points out, changes do show up in the color and texture of the human iris. As new tissue replaces old tissue it can be evaluated by the medical doctor. "It is impossible to tell from the eyes what germ life exists in the body, but when tissues have degenerated to the stage where germ life exists in various parts of the body, it will be reflected in the iris," says Dr. Jensen.

It was this system that Dr. Herman Saussele practiced with all of his patients, prescribing either homeopathic remedies, dietetic supplements, or chiropractic adjustments, as the case might be.

Does it work? Eugene C. Henkel, Jr., father of five children and a railroad ticket office clerk, visited Dr. Saussele in October, 1953. At the time Henkel was, at age forty-nine, hunchbacked; he had a stiff neck; he could not raise his arms over his head; and he was unable to drive to work. He had been told by an orthodox M.D. to get a wheelchair. Dr. Saussele's iris diagnosis revealed that the patient had in the past suffered various respiratory disturbances, a matter that was immediately verified. Dr. Saussele prescribed a treatment consisting of special foods, vitamins, food supplements, and exercises. Today Henkel drives about fifty thousand miles a year in connection with his own business. He is still somewhat stiff and somewhat stoop shouldered, but no longer crippled or in pain.

Mrs. Agnes Ludbeck visited Dr. Saussele on April 24, 1961, when she was fifty-five years old. She had been under medical treatment for high blood pressure, which Dr. Saussele found to be 206 over 110. Mrs. Ludbeck had been to an eye specialist for trouble in her eyes. The specialist had treated her for two years but had assured her that there was nothing wrong with her except atmospheric pressure. She herself wondered if there was some systemic condition, but he reassured her and advised her to keep putting drops into her eyes and not to worry about it. On examination Dr. Saussele found this patient to suffer from diabetes and a blood sugar count of 254 milligrams (the normal limit is 120 mgs.). The woman came to see Dr. Saussele once a week and received supplements for liver and pancreas treatment.

A year later she quit her job and retired to Troy, Missouri. At that time her blood pressure was down to 158 over 84 and her blood sugar to 158 mgs. But being away from Dr. Saussele's care did something to her system. Two years later she was hospitalized in Troy, unable to walk. Her disease was diagnosed as diabetic neuritis. Friends brought her back to St. Louis and Dr. Saussele. Three days after he started treatment, the woman began to limp around by herself; three weeks later she was fine.

Richard Janson came to Dr. Saussele's attention on November 5, 1963, at age eighteen. He then weighed 72 pounds and was very much debilitated. The boy had been in and out of medical hospitals without success. Dr. Saussele started to work on the boy at Christmas, 1963. Because of the young man's condition, the doctor had to go to his house to treat him, but Dr. Saussele's healing worked so well that the young man was able to go back to school by May, 1964, and to graduate. Unfortunately, he had a relapse and Saussele had to start all over again.

The doctor discovered then that certain psychosomatic factors had also come into play. He began to re-educate the young man's thinking, preaching a positive mental attitude and referring him to a classic book on the subject, Claude M. Bristol's *The Magic of Believing*. By fall of the same year the young man was able to get a job.

Dr. Saussele saw him every week until October, 1965. When Dr. Saussele next saw the young man, at Christmas, 1967, when the boy was home on leave from the U.S. Navy, he weighed 142 pounds.

After I had learned of Dr. Saussele's work, I had arranged to visit his office to submit to his iris diagnosis. Of course, he knew nothing of my medical history. He put me in his chair and examined my eyes carefully. Employing a large magnifying glass, he scrutinized my eyes minutely, jotting down his findings as he went along. Each sector of the iris represents a different part of the human system, iridologists claim, and according to the coloring and shape of a particular part of the iris, Dr. Saussele drew certain conclusions.

"You have a thyroid condition," he said. "I can see it right here in your eye." I nodded. I had been under treatment for a sluggish thyroid gland for years and was at this time taking half a grain of thyroid extract twice a day.

The doctor shone a light into my eyes, in order to get a reflex reaction. "This is a gastric reflex, and here we have a gall bladder reflex and a liver reflex. In other words you have a nervous digestive system." I nodded an emphatic yes. "And a nervous stomach." Again I nodded. Dr. Saussele's iridological findings were absolutely true.

Healing is the major component of the teaching of the late "sleeping prophet" Edgar Cayce, about whom many books have been written and whose great work is being carried on by his sons at the Association for Research and Enlightenment (ARE) in Virginia Beach, Virginia. Cayce, an untutored photographer, went into trance states during which he was able to diagnose the illnesses of people about whom he knew nothing. The language and contents of these diagnoses were such that only a trained medical doctor could have undertaken them. Nevertheless, Edgar Cayce had no such training nor was there any fraud or delusion involved. Many of the prescriptions given to the thousands of people who sought Cayce's help turned out to be unknown to the orthodox medical fraternity. Nevertheless, these remedies all worked and much was learned by those willing to learn from the study of the Cayce records.

Today, Cayce's diagnoses in specific cases are carefully filed away for those who wish to consult them when similar diseases require it. Those joining ARE obtain the so-called Black Book, a list of the most common diseases and a record of what Edgar Cayce prescribed in individual cases as remedies. Connected with the Association for Research and Enlightenment in Virginia Beach, Virginia, is a pharmacy specializing in Edgar Cayce prescriptions: the Heritage Store, P.O. Box 77, Virginia Beach, Virginia 23458. Items for sale are prepared under strict supervision of the ARE authorities and tie in with specific recommendations or prescriptions made by the late seer. From personal experience I can state that such prescriptions have, not infrequently, proved amazingly effective where conventional medicines have failed me.

Because this is a controversial program, ARE has always maintained close liaison with medical doctors friendly toward their cause—for example, in a recent symposium called the Triune Concept of Healing, held in New York, Edith Wallace, M.D., and Robert G. Brewer, M.D., discussed the Cayce concept of healing as it applied to conventional medicine—because ARE believes that in a combination of Cayce's prescriptions with the methods and prestige of establishment medicine lies the greatest hope for mass acceptance of the Cayce teachings.

As a first step in that direction, ARE maintains a special clinic in Phoenix, Arizona, where medical doctors treat patients with reference to the Edgar Cayce material. The clinic is housed in a pleasant suburb of Phoenix, with the mountains as backdrop. It consists of a complex of one-story buildings and a small garden. By no means comparable to a hospital or a large research establishment, the clinic is nevertheless run along orthodox lines in the sense that patients are seen by appointment, medical records are kept, and the entire operation is undertaken with the full approval and blessing of Arizona medical authorities.

Established in early 1970, the clinic had from the beginning been the special project of Dr. William McGarey and the ARE Board of Trustees. Dr. McGarey lives in Phoenix, the climate is favorable for the treatment of a number of diseases, and the atmosphere is unhurried and free from the sort of pressures prevalent in large metropolitan centers.

On a visit to the Phoenix center, I discussed the program with the manager, McCaleb.

"How did the ARE hope to benefit the world by establishing this clinic?" I asked him.

"More than 50 percent of the Cayce readings are physical readings. Studying those readings, we try to verify them and learn from them."

"How does this work as far as patients are concerned?"

"First of all, we have to take all the readings on a specific disease and study them. It takes about an hour per reading to synthesize this material and come up with what we think the source of the readings is trying to work from, what attitude or basic laws are involved. Then we come up with a general prescription or a therapy approach for the disease and apply it to a group of patients and see how it works; we modify as we go along."

"In other words, the patients coming here are being treated by methods prescribed by Cayce previously for similar cases?"

"Correct. Modified in some cases by the doctor's own knowledge."

"What range of disease is being treated here? Is there any limitation?" I asked.

"There are 233 diagnoses that have been discovered in the readings of what we would call separate diseases. We've only started to work on a few of these; it will take a bigger staff to get to all of them."

"Are there any diseases that have not been touched at all?"

"Yes. While we have a young intern studying the readings on cancer, we have not yet tried to deal with it."

"What are the principal diseases you deal with?"

"Epilepsy, myasthenia gravis, spearodermia, arthritis."

"You say there should be a larger staff. Do

you have any assistants?"

"We have fifteen full-time people and five part-time people working here. Our limitation is strictly financial. The main source of our finding comes from seeing general practice patients. The doctors work here at a decreased personal salary and the difference goes into building up the staff; we're adding new doctors as fast as we can generate the funds to put them on the payroll."

"How many M.D.s. do you have on the staff?"

"Four."

"Are they specialists or general practitioners?"

"Dr. McGarey is a specialist in Cayce's approaches, and of course in neurological diseases, particularly multiple sclerosis. We have a specialist in obstetrics and gynecology; Dr. Gladys McGarey, a general practitioner; and Dr. Arthur Wright, who is a general practitioner who came to us from New Hampshire, and who also understands the general thrust of the Cayce readings. He's here learning to apply that to his medical practice."

"How does the American Medical Association feel about your enterprise? Do you have any problems with them?"

"No. Our doctors are members in good standing; for example, the McGareys have a long association with the county medical society here. This was another reason for being in Phoenix. Had we picked up the McGareys and moved them to Virginia Beach, there might have been some trouble with the medical association there. Here everybody knows the McGareys as good, reputable doctors, and no one is concerned with the fact that they are doing something a little unorthodox."

"Do you cooperate with hospitals in the area?"

"Our doctors are on the staff of several hospitals, and they put patients into them when the occasion arises."

"Are you publishing anything applying to this particular clinic?"

"Dr. McGarey has just had an article published in the county magazine on healing around the world. We're just starting our second year of the *Medical Research Bulletin*, which goes, free of charge, to all our cooperating doctors and is available for subscription to lay people."

"Who are the cooperating doctors?"

"The cooperating doctors are those who have indicated a desire to receive information from the ARE. They fall into two categories: those who simply want to receive the information, and those who are also willing to take ARE patients who wish to have a Cayce style treatment rather than a standard medical approach."

"Where are these doctors located?"

"All over the country."

"Can you name one or two."

"Dr. Fred Lancer in Chattanooga; Dr. Robert Forbess, a dermatologist in San Diego. There are approximately two hundred M.D.'s and D.O.'s. participating. Also, around six hundred chiropractors."

"How many of them are pure M.D.'s?"

"Around a hundred pure M.D.'s."

"How many patients a week are seen here at the clinic?"

"Each doctor is working a full schedule, between twenty-five and thirty-five hours of actual patient time each week. A standard unit is fifteen minutes. Consultations take half an hour; complete physicals take an hour and a half. Our complete physical is as complete as any you can get in a general practice office."

"Is there a lab connected with this clinic?"

"We have a small lab for routine work. There is a lab here in town that we send most of our work out to, Arizona Health Labs."

"How are the patients charged?"

"The fees are, in general, the standard fee for medical treatment in the city of Phoenix."

"There are no extra charges for being treated with ARE methods?"

"No, we try to hold our fees down. We are charging a hundred dollars for a complete work up and that is considered fairly low."

"Suppose somebody wants to come here and has no funds?"

"We are currently collecting what we call the 'Indigent Patient Funds.' As times goes on, we will be able to take on indigent patients who have a serious need and who fit into research programs. I might add that when we go into our arthritis project—when there will be fifty patients treated here and fifty 'controls' treated at another clinic —our fifty patients will not be charged."

"Do you work with Blue Cross and any other

organization along those lines?"

"Our insurance policy is standard. We have a full-time insurance girl who fills out the forms for our patients regardless of what insurance company they deal with."

"Have you ever supplemented the Cayce readings with related material from other sources?"

"There is a great interest on the part of our doctors for all types of healing. However, the Cayce material has so much breadth and depth that it is going to be many years before we can get too far beyond a level of simple interest."

"Do your doctors go outside the clinic to treat patients?"

"We do make house calls on our regular patients who need it."

I thanked the manager for his time and went over to Dr. William McGarey's office. The doctor turned out to be a pleasant, soft-spoken gentleman who worded his replies to my questions carefully and, perhaps understandably—after all, it isn't every day that you can question an M.D. and a member of the AMA on his work in psychic healing.

"Dr. McGarey, how many years have you been interested in the Cayce readings?" I began.

"I've been in the ARE since 1957."

"When did the idea strike you to use the material from the readings in your practice?"

"Almost at once, because I looked at these ideas and thought, if Cayce can search a person's unconscious mind, then there must be some basis for understanding it. When you first read the Cayce material, it is confusing to the medical mind because he talks in strange terms. He talks about 'coagulation' when he means 'cell construction.' In the practice of medicine we don't even *think* of cell construction."

"Do you think that the source which gave Cayce his information was medically trained?"

"I think the source was Cayce's unconscious mind reaching out and contacting the unconscious mind of other people. Cayce had the past life experience of having been a healer himself, back in Persia, thousands of years ago."

"Do you feel that there is an understanding of medical technology, medical terminology in the readings?"

"To a certain degree."

"Is it beyond what he as a conscious person would have known?"

"Yes." Dr. McGarey was emphatic.

"Do you find that any of this material could be derived from the minds of discarnate physicians?"

"Some of it, but not all of it."

"You refer to strange expressions. Are they strange in the use of words, or strange because of the ideas expressed by them?"

"Strange in the use of words. The ideas expressed are physiological ideas. The difference, I think, between the way he talks about the body and the way doctors and other people think about it is the difference between function and structure. Cayce talks as if a function is a real entity. In other words, a function is a living, active process and maybe function actually creates structure. The way he looks at it, an individual is a *spiritual* being *first* and manifests, through mind, as a *material* being. If this is true, then the spirit creates and the physical body is the result. If this is so, the spiritual being is the function, or the power, or the life force, and the physical structure, all parts of it, are there in order to let that life force manifest. Therefore, this structure is a result of function or of life. The function becomes the life process. The structure is just a means whereby it can express itself.

"In medicine we think in terms of *structure*. We think this man has liver disease, or lung disease, or his heart is abnormal, or he has brain disease, or he has an appendix that is inflamed. The way Cayce talks about it, one of the forces within the body has become unbalanced with the other forces, a system is out of coordination with another system, or the liver is not coordinating in its function with the kidneys because they're both eliminatory organs and the function of elimination has to come about or the individual dies. It is a different aproach from the standpoint of function, and the way we *currently* think about it, the structure is the thing we go by."

"How do *you* feel about it? Who is right?"

Dr. McGarey did not pause for a second.

*"Oh, I think Cayce is right,"* he said.

"Would you define then the approach to healing using this, shall we say, progressive medicine?"

"I don't think it is a progressive stance toward medicine, since it hails back to the way Cayce did it ten thousand years ago in Persia. It is as ancient as man. I've come to call it *physiological rehabilitation*. Physiology is the study of the functioning of the parts of the body, the parts that keep the body alive."

"Are you using Cayce's recommendations as to medicine and treatments?"

"I'm using the principles he talked about, not the specific medications. I think he was talking in principles. He would have someone get a series of colonics and have another person take castor oil, or Epsom salt baths, then he'd have another person take a massage for the same purpose—to stimulate the eliminations of the body."

"But you will adopt the method according to the needs of the individual patient, is that right?"

"That's right."

"What about some of the substances Cayce does prescribe that are at variance with the accepted methods of treatment for these diseases?"

"It depends on what you're comparing it to. For instance, in arthritis we use atomadine, which is a type of iodine preparation. Iodine is used in medicine all the time, as in drops of SSKI (saturated solution potassium iodine). But the atomadine Cayce suggests is an iodine trichloride solution. He says that iodine stimulates all the glands of the body to function more normally. It acts as a cleansing agent and an aid to the function of the cells. Atomadine used over a period of time builds up, and that is the way I use it, in ascending dosages from one drop a day up to five drops, which is still a minimal amount. Then he says use an Epsom salts bath to eliminate *through the skin,* which is an eliminatory organ. Eliminate some of the toxins. Some people in medicine, especially the physical therapists, use all sorts of physical therapy methods to combat arthritis. But the difference is this: I believe that arthritis is just a result of the body malfunctioning. If I can get the body functioning property, arthritis will *not* be present. Aspirin used to contain the disease is not a cure."

"Do you feel the same way about cancer?"

"I have not researched cancer, and so I'm not sure what Cayce said about cancer. He did say there were nine different kinds. With leukemia, he said that tincture of iodine taken and mixed with blood drawn from the patient and then injected back in would cure maybe 50 percent of the cases of non-acidic leukemia."

"Has this ever been done?"

"No. Because he said first of all you have to test it in animals in order to determine the dosage and determine the side effects and so it has never been done. There is a good reason—no money."

"What diseases do you specialize in here?"

"We work with arthritis and respiratory diseases, the usual thing that you see in a general practitioner's office."

"You don't concern yourself with physical disease, accidents, and things of that sort?"

"Not so much, although the healing of the body after an accident is much improved if you pay attention to the functions of the body."

"Have you done any work with mental patients?"

"Some. We have psychiatrists cooperating with the Edgar Cayce Research Foundation Program, and some are using Cayce's suggestions on schizophrenia."

"Which area do you feel strongest in?"

"I would be equally divided between respiratory diseases and arthritis, spearodermia, and pelvic diseases of women, which, I think, respond very well to Cayce's suggestions."

"Do you ever get involved with vitamins or other forms of dietary treatments?"

"Not vitamin treatments, diet treatments as such. We're working with a human being who is a manifestation of spirit. We're trying to bring that person to a wholeness. If we give a lot of vitamins to cure arthritis, then we may be avoiding a real confrontation of the human being."

"You are trying to heal the *whole* organism even though only *part* of it is affected."

"I think it is *all* affected. Cayce said that the body, the mind, and the spirit are one. If they are one, then a kink in one is a kink in another."

"Do you have any work with hypnosis?"

"No."

"Do you do any work involving the aura?"

"No. I'm interested, but I don't see the aura."

"Are you aware of the implication of auric treatments?"

"Yes."

"Is there any plan to develop that?"

"Yes, but it is in the future. I think that we need gradually to orient doctors in this whole field of parapsychology as such, the activity of the spiritual nature of man as it affects medical practice. I think doctors will *have* to become acquainted with it or they'll pass into oblivion."

"Do you perform surgery here?" I said, changing the subject again.

"Minor surgery. If someone cuts their hand, I sew it up. Or taking off little cysts or something of that nature."

"Isn't that in contradiction of Cayce's ideas on wholeness?"

"No, he said that if you have castor oil consciousness, use castor oil, and, to paraphrase that, if you have surgery consciousness, use surgery. Some people are in a state of awareness where surgery is the thing that they need at this time, this place."

"Are there any surgeons operating under the Cayce directive?"

"Yes. There's one in Bethesda, Maryland, Dr. Robert Brewer. He's going to be on our symposium next year. This is the fifth time. We are also having Dr. Ernie Petche, who is a psychiatrist from California, and William Tiller, who was head of the Department of Material Sciences at Stanford University, a physicist."

"In your treatment do you ever have reference to prior incarnations as being, in some way, connected with diseases?"

"Sure, because people who come to me understand about reincarnation and it makes treatment a whole lot simpler. I think that whether reincarnation happens or not, it is much more reasonable to think in terms of it than not and so you can explain and understand things and thus act in accordance with reason a lot better if you know that something may be *karmic* in its origin."

"Do you yourself accept the karmic origin of much disease?"

"Yes."

"Is there some way of evaluating the karmic element in disease and thus of reversing the process?"

"I think so. I think that the karmic element almost always comes from manifestation of glandular malfunction."

"In understanding the cause do you feel that the disease can be checked?"

"Sometimes. It depends, I think, on what the person has chosen even before he is born. If he were born without limbs, this is a *karmic* affliction. We don't know enough yet to help a person grow new limbs, although the potential is there. Potential is in each cell of the human body, and this has been demonstrated by physicians who do research. But that kind of karmic affliction may be something he has chosen to live with through a whole incarnation."

"Have you had any personal problems with the American Medical Association because of your views and your work?"

"I had one case, when I was giving a lecture and the people in that city got overenthusiastic and sent announcements to all the doctors. The president of their society wrote a letter to the secretary of our society and said, 'What about this guy talking about the unconscious mind? Is he some kind of a nut?' and our secretary wrote back and said, 'No. He's got ideas of his own and he's a respected member of the medical community.'"

I was deeply impressed with Dr. McGarey's sincerity and level-headed approach to the problem at hand: how to reconcile orthodox medical training with the Edgar Cayce teachings. Quite obviously the two are on a collision course. If the doctor is right in supporting the Cayce view of man, and I am convinced that he is, then much of what he was taught in medical school can no longer be true. For instance, the traditional view of the body as a superior animal, developed through the long and arduous process of evolution from lower animal forms, and essentially subject to the laws of the physical universe only, is diametrically opposed to the teachings of Cayce and most other esoteric teachers, that the physical is merely an expression of the spiritual and that the spiritual has created the physical manifestation, not vice versa.

Surely, an entirely new form of medicine lies just beyond the horizon. Fortunately the Association for Research and Enlightenment in Virginia Beach and in the many branches throughout the United States is doing everything within its power to shed additional light upon these amazing teachings of a man without medical training, without superior knowledge and, for that matter, without any ambitions to be anything but a humble vehicle.

The clinic at Phoenix is merely one attempt

to acquaint the general public with the Cayce material and to use it in a practical way to heal the sick. On still another level, physical therapy, Harold J. Reilly, of New Jersey, has been active in the field of body conditioning and rehabilitating through exercise and a planned program of physical activity. What makes the Reilly method different from any other form of physiotherapy is of course his relationship with the late Edgar Cayce.

"One of the most interesting and intriguing experiences I have had is that of helping to condition hundreds of men and women referred to me by the famous miracle man of Virginia Beach, the well-known psychic, Edgar Cayce. For about two years before I had even met the man, and continuing seventeen years after until his death, he advised people to come to me for conditioning. As this advice was given in a trance state I felt curiously honored to have been selected from out of the ether to give a special type of therapy I was already using for general conditioning. I was further flattered when this strangely gifted man came in for my personal manipulations," writes Harold Reilly in one of his books, *Easy Does It*. Reilly preaches physical conditioning as a philosophy of life. To him, the health and function of muscles, glands, organs, mind, and *spirit* all depend on the movements of the body. Many public figures, Hollywood stars, and sportsmen have used Reilly's services over the years. Many came to Reilly to improve their figures, to lose excess weight, or to have their health restored when under stress, but many others came because Reilly was the man to see if one was interested in the Edgar Cayce philosophy of life. Somehow Harold Reilly, who holds a doctorate in chiropractics, is the physical exponent of the Cayce teachings. After a patient has been ministered to by someone practicing on the basis of the Cayce readings, he is frequently sent to the Reilly clinic for a combination of rest and toning up. Up to June, 1960, Reilly handled about 1,000 cases referred to him by the Edgar Cayce foundation. He arranged for treatments in his drugless therapy field for patients requiring osteopathy, chiropractic massage, hydrotherapy, homeotherapy, and other forms of treatment requiring no drugs whatsoever.

As Dr. Reilly reported in the *Searchlight*, a publication of ARE, the patients sent to him fell into four categories: those having to do with the increase of circulation, those having to do with the increase in the elimination, those having to do with relaxation, and those having to do with the proper approach to eating. Harold Reilly was able to show them the way to better health, but to maintain good health, patients were required to continue a balanced program of specific exercises at all times.

So great was and is Edgar Cayce's impact on the American scene that it was perhaps inevitable that people, sooner or later, would claim to be carrying on the work of the late seer of Virginia Beach. Well-meaning psychics and not so well-meaning opportunists have come forward to claim contact with Edgar Cayce. "Get help now from Dr. Ernesto A. Montgomery, the West Indies prophet.

Not since the great Edgar Cayce has so amazing a prophet and healer appeared," is the somewhat all-encompassing statement put forward by a well-known Los Angeles psychic reader.

Two housewives in Cincinnati, Ohio, who have worked together for years in what they believe to be a contact with the late Edgar Cayce, I have investigated carefully myself. One of the two women, the medium, received "Cayce's messages" in trance; the other took them down for posterity. As with all such messages, I take great care to differentiate between the patently false or erroneous and the possibly genuine. In the case of the two ladies in Cincinnati, the alleged Cayce speaking to me through the entranced medium was unable to answer a number of key questions put to him. The information had been supplied to me by Hugh Lyn Cayce, son of the late Edgar, and included names and situations that could have been answered only by the authentic Edgar Cayce.

Similarly, a dentist in the Middle West laid claim to being a mouthpiece for the late Edgar Cayce. Despite her apparent sincerity and conviction that she was indeed the chosen one, none of the material obtained through her can be verified sufficiently to support her claim.

It would appear that Edgar Cayce will choose his mouthpiece very carefully so as not to create conflict or doubt in the minds of researchers as to the genuineness of the communications. Thus far no one has come forward with sufficient evidence to support a claim of being the mouthpiece of the late Edgar Cayce. This may yet happen in the future, and when it occurs, it will benefit humankind beyond belief; for if the incarnate Edgar Cayce was able to prescribe medications for thousands of people, relying only on the knowledge given him in trance by discarnates, how much greater must the knowledge of the discarnate now be, after he himself has crossed the threshold into the world of spirit and become acquainted with its laws and truths.

At this writing, the Cayce Foundation's ARE Clinic in Phoenix, Arizona, is a firmly established alternative center, with Drs. Gladys and William McGarey still at the helm. Those wishing to avail themselves of their counsel or services should contact the Association for Research and Enlightenment (ARE) at P.O. Box 595, Virginia Beach, VA 23451. There is also a holistic pharmacy connected with the Association where Cayce-inspired medicines may be obtained at reasonable prices.

Probably one of the most brilliant and innovative medical pioneers is John C. Pierrakos, M.D., researcher and practicing psychiatrist in New York City. Dr. Pierrakos, in his treatise, *The Energy Field in Man and Nature*, establishes through experimentation the existence of energy fields in humans, plants, and even crystals—thus seriously endangering the cherished notion that the world is divided into organic and inorganic matter. The treatise was published by his Institute of Bioenergetic Analysis, at 71 Park Avenue in New York City. Because the human energy field (or aura) consists of three separate layers, healing of the various layers, that is the application of a healer's own powers to the field, presents a rational, if unorthodox, explanation in respect to the question of how psychic healing works.

"The field phenomena are related to the energy metabolism of the body," writes Dr. Pierrakos, "its production of heat, emotional excitement, rate and quality of breathing, activity, and rest. They are also affected by atmospheric conditions, relative humidity, polarity of charges in the air, and many other unknown factors."

It is clear that the inclusion of this knowledge in the treatment of the ill, even by conventional means, is likely to alter the conservative outlook of the average physician. But for the vast majority of medical practitioners to accept Dr. Pierrakos's findings would mean relearning and rethinking much, an effort human nature seems to resist with most people. But those in need of, or seriously interested in, this approach to human nature and healing, might want to consult the doctor him or herself.

Another eminent psychiatrist, Dr. Ralph Dickson Yaney, has found the inclusion of reincarnation material in the treatment of his psychoanalytical cases of great value. He uses reputable psychics to obtain past life material about clients and astrological charts, to gain a better insight into his patients' personalities. Whether the reincarnation material is factual or not, it appears that its use in the psychoanalytic process can be quite positive. Dr. Yaney is extremely careful in his selection of sensitives (psychics), and quite knowledgeable in astrology: he uses professional astrological character analysis based on birth, not any kind of fortunetelling. One may debate the methods he uses, but more and more psychiatrists are employing such alternative techniques (as did Carl Jung in his applications of astrology). In fact, in my conversations with several of Dr. Yaney's patients, they all indicated that they were indeed helped by the insights gained from these alternative sources.

For those interested in additional information about alternative medical treatments, *The Healthview Newsletter* is a periodical publication supported by a number of natural-healing oriented physicians, dentists and chiropractors. It is published at 612 Rio Road West, Box 6670, Charlottesville, VA 22906.

# HEALING AND THE OCCULT SCIENCES

## (Beyond Medicine)

The concept of psychic and unorthodox healing has always been part and parcel of all occult teachings, no matter what specific philosophy was involved, whether Western or Eastern in origin. No esoteric concept is imaginable unless the healing of body, mind, and spirit is also involved. The separation of material and spiritual things, or of body versus mind as it is practiced in Western thought and orthodox medicine, is totally alien to the occult sciences, which view humankind as a whole, the components of which are inseparable and indivisible.

Wrongful thoughts create illnesses, and thought processes reverse the conditions. Such matters are entirely in the hands of the sufferer—no one is forced to think wrongfully, and once the mistakes are realized, a person is capable of reversing the trend.

There is no superior power in operation to prevent one from seeing the light and doing something about one's condition. The act of acquiring knowledge, of looking into a problem of health, of initiating a process of healing, is a voluntary act on the part of the patient. The results of this act are not necessarily guaranteed: the patient may or may not succeed in locating a proper healer, and the healer may or may not succeed in helping the condition. In the case of self-healing, the sufferer may or may not succeed in his efforts, even if he applies himself thoroughly and according to the techniques he has learned. According to the law of karma, free will is that which we exercise upon our own judgment, whether motivated by emotional or logical factors. What we accomplish by our own decision will of course affect the final outcome—in various ways, depending upon the abilities and powers of the individual to carry out a determined course. But the condition requiring some action on our part is not entirely of our own making. According to the philosophy of reincarnation, of which the law of karma is a part, conditions are in existence independent of us. We move toward them or become involved with them in order to react to them, rather than the other way around. According to this widely held belief, illness may result from wrongful thinking, or from a variety of causes as in accidents, but the causative factors were brought together by the law of karma, which required such a condition to exist at that point in our lives.

Generally unaware of this influence around us, we then proceed to deal with the situation as it arises and in the best way we know. Thus we control the *outcome* to a large degree; we do not control the *incident*, which is determined by a superior law and order.

We may ask ourselves, why do some people become ill in certain ways, while others living under similar circumstances do not. To say simply that wrongful thinking in this particular case has caused disease is not sufficient. Why did such and such an individual think wrongfully, thus causing disease? Why was he not led to sources of information that would have prevented his wrongful thinking while someone else, under similar cirtumstances, was helped to find the information that would prevent his having wrongful thoughts? What determines the fate of the individual, the destiny that begins and ends with the state of health?

According to the philosophy of reincarnation, widely accepted in the eastern part of our globe and among many esoteric people in the West as well, one's previous incarnation and what one accomplished during it determines progress in the current one. One works out through ill health what one committed in a previous lifetime. For example, crippled individuals or those with birth defects are believed to have been culprits of one kind or another in another lifetime, causing others to become crippled or injured in similar, though not necessarily identical, ways.

This belief postulates a law of retribution in which the wrongs of one lifetime must be worked out by the right doings of another. The problem is that the average person is not aware of his previous lifetimes and thus has no way of focusing his actions in such a way that he can undo the wrong of a previous incarnation *consciously*. He must do so purely out of his own initiative, intuitively. By doing something correctly in the current incarnation, without knowing why one does so, the individual cancels out an ancient debt.

On those rare occasions when people have snatches of memory of previous lives, they are permitted this "bonus" because a previous lifetime had been cut short or been tragic in some other way. To the extent of these bits and pieces of information they are able to check back upon earlier incarnations and learn, perhaps even profit, from such memories. But unless these individuals work with a reputable hypnotist to regress them and dredge up from their unconscious the deeply embedded memories of past lives, they will be unable to make much practical use of that information. By and large, people do not recall previous lives, and those purporting to supply "life readings," going into great detail over dozens of former lives, are perhaps only dealing in hopes, if not outright fantasies.

Genuine reincarnation memories are of the kind that contain names, places, and details that are capable of verification in historical records. Fantasy reports on previous lives frequently include fanciful countries, nonexistent names, or conditions that cannot be properly checked out. This is not to say that some of these life readings do not contain true information as well, but one must use extreme caution in accepting material from earlier incarnations, especially if one tends to base one's present activities upon them.

## Healing and the Occult Sciences / 171

In accepting karmic causes for specific diseases, we are not necessarily forced to live with them as incurable or unalterable. The fact that the disease exists in this incarnation only means that something caused it to be in a past lifetime: what we do about it in this life is our own concern, and we are quite free to do everything within our power to relieve the condition.

Simply by having the condition in the first place, karmic law has been satisfied. Once that is so, an individual may use esoteric or orthodox methods to rid him or herself of the condition without affecting karmic law in the least; for it is no human's destiny to suffer with or without cause. To suffer with cause is unnecessary if one recognizes the cause and does something about it, and to suffer without cause, when there is no recognizable reason for it, is even less acceptable, for in such cases the absence of any notion of guilt makes the healing effort so much more plausible.

Psychic healing, of course, is in itself part of the occult sciences; the majority of mediums, whether professional or amateur, have some healing gift and are able to perform healings—largely because the force that makes healings possible is the same force that makes psychic phenomena in general possible. It may be utilized to make communications between the so-called dead and the living available to those seeking them, or it may be used in one of several ways as the driving power behind physical phenomena, clairvoyance, psychometry, and the entire range of ESP phenomena. The choice is the user's.

Although astrology is not strictly part of the occult sciences, it is frequently considered an allied art and those interested in psychic phenomena are nearly always also interested in astrology. Basically, however, astrology relies on mathematical considerations, on conclusions drawn from certain positions in the heavens and on earth, rather than on any intuitive, emotional processes. However, astrology has long held that certain planets "rule" or influence and dominate certain parts of the human body and mind, and if we accept the validity of astrology on the basis that it represents cosmic radiation primarily from the nearby planets, the sun, and our moon, then this concept does acquire scientific validity. Cosmic radiation bombards our earth at all times, is measurable, and can be evaluated as to possible results. Some cosmic radiation is definitely harmful whether of natural or synthetic origin. Other radiation is beneficial, and astrology has pinpointed these effects and placed them in the appropriate relationship to the human personality.*

Basically, there are two relationships to consider when one deals with the astrological impact upon one's health. First, the astrological chart of the individual at the time of *birth* reflects the strength and weakness of the individual, the areas in which he or she *may* expect trouble, and the

---

*Those who wish to acquaint themselves with exact data for each and every part of the body according to the twelve zodiac signs will find profuse and detailed information in such works as Carroll Righter's *Your Astrological Guide to Health and Diet*. Sybil Leek also has written extensively on the relationship between health and astrology.

areas in which he or she may not. Certain planets "rule" certain parts of the body; thus the parts of the body so ruled will be strongly affected when these planets are in certain positions. If the positions are in a "friendly position" to the rest of the person's horoscope, then beneficial results will prevail and that part of the body will feel fine. Conversely, if the planets are badly related, illness in those areas is possible, though not necessarily inevitable. (Nothing in astrology is ever inevitable—especially if the person, by being forewarned, looks out for potential difficulties and tries to avoid them.)

Second, the "aspects," or relationships between individual planets, the sun, and the moon *at certain times* in the current life of the person involved, also have a lot to do with the state of health at that time. While the natal chart—the horoscope at the time of birth—reflects permanent and basic conditions in the organism, the temporal configurations in the heavens relate to the state of health at specific times in the life of the individual.

No one should follow the advice of a brief newspaper column on what to do on a certain day, as such material is neither scientific nor accurate. But careful scrutiny of an individual chart drawn by a competent astrologer for the person involved will disclose certain trends existing at certain times. One should study these conditions and then make one's decisions as to what one might do under those "transits" and what not. A calm, rational approach to astrological data can be utilized to preserve one's good health and prevent accidents.

Somewhat on the fringes of the occult sciences are the various forms of yoga. These teachings of Indian and Tibetan philosophers are very ancient and very basic. Hatha yoga, dealing with the physical body, is particularly valuable to those living a life according to esoteric concepts. Hatha yoga should take the place of ordinary calisthenics or gymnastics. The principal difference between this yoga and all other forms of exercise is simply expressed. In ordinary exercise, body parts—muscles, limbs, and breathing apparatus—are used rapidly or consecutively in order to test their abilities. Doing twenty push-ups in the morning leaves one exhausted. Running as fast as one is able is equally ill-advised in many cases. Lifting weights beyond one's capacity may be dangerous. Playing tennis or handball, if one is not really used to it, causes undue strain on ligaments, wrists, and ankles and results in fatigue rather than in a strengthening of the bodily apparatus.

In yoga, on the other hand, emphasis is not on performance but on the holding of certain positions for as long as one is able. By taking on certain carefully designed positions and staying in those positions for a few seconds, gradually adding seconds until one accomplishes the maximum suggested by the teacher, one gives the affected muscle or limb a chance to expand without also using up precious energy. The secret of Hatha yoga lies in the calm and deliberate holding of positions. At the same time emphasis is put on the right frame of mind accompanying these positions and breathing at a comparable rate is also very much emphasized. Breath is the essence of life itself: many of the yoga exercises stress improved breathing techniques because the oxygen introduced into the lungs materially affects the operation of the body during the position.

Calisthenics and other forms of gymnastics as well as most ordinary sports pay no attention to mental or—heaven forbid—spiritual attitudes during the performances. Yoga, on the other hand, is effective only if mind and body coordinate their activities completely. By stressing this duality of purpose, yoga recognizes and utilizes the interaction of the physical and etheric bodies simultaneously and for mutual benefit.

Lastly, certain pagan religions, such as Wicca, stress healing among their most urgent goals. In Wicca, healing those present in the circle or those at a distance is accomplished by a community effort called the raising of the "cone of power." Energy is drawn from the participants through singing, chanting, and dancing in unison. As the energy potential becomes higher and higher, and just when it reaches the zenith of its power, the community is ordered to stop abruptly, usually dropping to the floor. By this abrupt action, the energy cone is released and sent forth in a predetermined direction. I have seen this method work repeatedly and know that energies thus produced and sent out to an ailing person can affect the state of health of the individual.

Such practices do in no way involve miracles or even strong belief on the part of the recipient. They are primarily scientifically acceptable tranfers of energies raised by a group of human beings for a single purpose. In some ways, this is a form of telepathy, except that thoughts of well-being are transmitted together with raw energy to burn out the diseased parts of the patient's aura.

Most likely some other emotionally tinged religions, such as the Holy Rollers, who work themselves up to fever pitch through religious singing and dancing, accomplish their healings in similar fashion. In either case, it is not necessarily the deity descending personally and touching the sick who performs the healing, but the religious practitioners themselves through the use and channeling of their bodily energies. The deity concept serves primarily as a focal power.

If the seemingly miraculous results are later ascribed to a supernatural agency, in a manner of speaking and indirectly that is correct; for if it were not for the concentration point represented by the deity symbol, the outpouring of energy would not have been accomplished.

Finally, some individuals wonder whether their illness may not be due to *psychic incursions*, that is, a kind of possession by external spirit entities, who bring with them an ailment from their own physical past.

It is perfectly true that mediums, especially the trance variety, take on the passing symptoms of the dead individual speaking through them or the sufferings and memories of illness that occurred in the life of the person using the medium at that moment. But these reenactments serve primarily to identify the individual and to exteriorize past sufferings in this way. After the trance state ends, nothing of the symptoms remains and the medium rarely remembers what went on while in trance. Ordinary individuals may become hosts to possessing entities in various ways, usually by permitting the contact either consciously or unconsciously, but the health condition of the possessor does not become a major factor unless the takeover is complete—in which case the host personality is in deep trouble all around and needs a good exorcist.

People who are sensitive may enter a place where sickness has been prevalent in the past and feel the "bad vibrations." This is a kind of psychometry, and a change of location usually ends the discomfort. True psychic incursions of the succubi or incubi variety (demons of either sex to the kabbalistically inclined) do not invade healthy, self-possessed individuals.

# WITCHCRAFT IS ALIVE AND WELL

## *(Pagans and Witches)*

It's Halloween and the party is in full swing. At least half a dozen guests are dressed up as witches, complete with wart on the nose, fright wig, crooked nose, black robe, pointed hat, and—naturally—the inevitable broomstick.

To the average person that's the image of a witch *today*.

Let's go back three hundred years, even two hundred years in some areas. A woman with ESP faculties has predicted the future accurately. Another woman is "speaking in strange tongues" while in a trance state. Still another one brews herbal teas that heal sicknesses the medical doctors can't touch. Why, they're all witches! Best thing to do with them, is burn 'em, because they're dangerous sorcerers in league with *The Devil!*

We still have psychic phenomena, but we don't call the women who experience them, *witches*. Three hundred years ago, the churches felt that anyone having these misunderstood gifts of ESP *had* to be evil, and consequently persecuted them cruelly. The image of the "ugly witch" is pure fiction, developed in the Middle Ages by fanatic priests (and laymen) as a means of destroying the remnants of "the old religion." Witchcraft, derived from "Wicca" (or Wisdom) was originally nothing more than the pre-Christian, pagan nature religion of many lands, especially the Celtic lands of Britain and Ireland, which reached their highest development in the Druidic priesthood. They had no truck with the devil as we understand the term today. In fact, the word devil derives from a Gypsy language expression, *Duvel*, meaning simply "Lord," and the phrase used by the witchcraft practitioners among the roaming Gypsies was "O boro duvel atch'pa leste" (translated as "May the great lord be with you"). To this day, the followers of Witchcraft greet each other with "Blessed be"—hardly words of evil.

Today, there are many *covens* or witchcraft communities in existence throughout the world. We don't read about them in the daily newspapers very often because first of all, the press does not take the Craft very seriously, and secondly, the members of the coven are sworn to secrecy during their initiation. Some outsiders have construed this as having evil meaning, but most lodges of freemasonry also impose this condition on their members. This is probably purely psychological, for it adds to the lure and excitement of belonging to a *select*, restricted group just like today's key clubs and other societies with snob appeal.

Today, more people than ever are interested in learning about Witchcraft, perhaps because

Christianity, Judaism or the other great religions have failed them, because they seek something more vital, more personal, in their lives than the orthodox faiths can give them.

Witchcraft is a very basic religion, accepting all initiates as equals before the altar, dispensing with dogma and hierarchy in favor of individual links with the deity through sensual and extrasensory release.

Small wonder that the Establishment churches fought the Craft, for Witchcraft is non-political, non-patriotic and not of this world. It is a pantheistic faith in the purest sense, under which all are truly as One.

I learned all about Witchcraft when I researched my three books dealing with it, and about the same time I received permission to make a unique documentary motion picture called "World of Witchcraft." Unique, in that I was allowed inside the secret meetings, even high level initiations and rituals. The motherland of Witchcraft is Britain, so I asked British Airways to get me over there: they did, figuring a lot of Americans might just want to follow me and find out about the Witches in England, too. Once the public relations people at British Airways realized how many people over here were interested in the occult (including Witchcraft), they even got me to the austere Board of Public Works, so I could get a permit to film at venerable Stonehenge—where my London friends would perform an actual Halloween ritual for my cameras. Because it was outdoors and raining, they kept their robes on. But the third degree initiation I was permitted to witness at Alex and Maxine Sanders' London temple was strictly in the buff: to tell the truth, I felt foolish with my clothes on. Since then I have gained a great deal of knowledge about this pagan cult, become an initiate myself (and caught a couple of colds at early spring outdoor rituals) and while I can't exactly consider myself the best spell-caster in the world, I enjoyed the mood and excitement of the covens very much. English Witches are polite and colorful, and definitely an "added attraction" if you go to Britain. But the native American groups (and they come in many traditions and variations) are warm and homey, and perhaps less stand-offish than their British cousins, because of the American character of openness: you can't become a "card-carrying Witch" just by applying, but if you're sincere you'll meet the "right" contacts before long; they will look you over for a year and a day, and then maybe you'll get the nod—though it can be sooner if you're what they want or need as a new member.

Witchcraft celebrates four main holidays, marking the changes of the seasons, since it is essentially a nature religion. These holidays are May Eve, April 30, the spring festival; Lammas, or the birth of summer, July 31; Halloween, really All Hallows' Eve, celebrating the coming of autumn and the harvest, always very important to witchcraft followers; and finally Brigid's Day, February 2nd, when the prettiest and youngest of the female witches is worshipped as a symbol of womanhood—a little like a beauty contest.

each full moon, at which time the members of the congregations go through a ritual together, watch a new member being initiated or just socialize with each other. The main holidays are called "sabbats," and the full moon festivities are referred to as "esbats." Both terms as well as some of the symbolism of the Craft are borrowed from the Hebrew kabbala or mystic tradition, but the basic rituals are Celtic in origin.

What exactly does go on when a coven of witches gets together?

A typical group of practicing believers in Cincinnati, Ohio, has 13 members; 7 men and 6 women. Their ages range from the early twenties to the fifties, and their professional identifications include that of artist, salesman, engineer, display designer, housewife, dancer, diver, secretary—no class distinctions in Witchcraft!

Because of the prevailing prejudices in our society against the occult in general, the coven maintains a certain secrecy and although the members know each other fully, only first names are used in their meetings. Moreover, it is witchcraft tradition to assume a *new name* for the practice of the Craft. Nothing sinister in that, either. All the popes do it, when they become Pope!

The meeting usually gets underway around 9 p.m. At first it is social, and the business of the coven follows next. Such prosaic pursuits as activities reports, dues collection and correspondence take up the early portion of the evening. At midnight, however, the circle begins. The "raising of the power" for some beneficial purpose—healing a member or friend via thought concentration, or influencing someone whose views are held harmful to humanity in some way—are among the goals. Does it work? Thought concentration is energy and can influence not only minds but objects, as Dr. Joseph Rhine proved at Duke University long ago. If it does not work, it certainly does no harm. And there is hardly a more spiritual community than a dedicated coven of "white" (or beneficial) witches. "Black covens" are an ilk of a different hue. These are people bent on thrills, borrowing from true Witchcraft, but perverted to pure destructiveness. They are the arch enemy of the true witches and should never be confused with them any more than Communism can be equated with the Catholic church.

The circle is formed by the members around a simple altar, with salt, representing earth; a chalice, symbolic of water; a candle, meaning fire; and a censer, symbolic of the element air, in the four quarters of the circle. The High Priest is in the center. The ritual then proceeds according to a manual called the *Book of Shadows*, a kind of witchcraft bible. Other sacred tools for the ceremony include a sword, symbol of worldly power, a dagger called an athame, a cord, a staff or wand, and a cauldron of water around which some covens dance and chant to raise their "spirits"—concentrations of energy. Everything in Witchcraft is symbolic and not to be taken literally. In fact, the fictional broomstick ride has some basis in that the symbolic straddling of a broomstick during the rite is an incentive to the grain to grow to that height.

is an incentive to the grain to grow to that height. After a carefully phrased ritual in which the "Guardians" of the four corners of the world are invoked to provide protection, wine is sipped symbolically, yoga-like breathing exercises are followed by protracted dancing around the altar, Virginia-reel style. In the end, everybody goes home exhausted, but relaxed.

Witchcraft followers have often been criticized for the performance of their rituals in the nude, and all sorts of gory fantasies are bandied about in fictional accounts of these practices. The truth is that they feel that their bodies are energy fields and clothes hamper the free flow of this body energy, but *some* covens, such as the one in Cincinnati, do wear long robes with nothing underneath.

Those most intrigued by the mysteries of Witchcraft are the young and women of many ages: the young, especially those in rebellion against the established forces in the world, see in Witchcraft a religion their elders can't share; they relish the special position that being Witches will give them in the community.

The current musical idiom, with its accompanying drug habits, is not so different from the frantic chanting and dancing of the Sabbat, and the unguent with which Witches of old used to anoint themselves for an imaginary "trip" to the Blocksberg is the direct precursor of LSD.

Witchcraft had its origin at the very dawn of humankind, long, long before there were Christians and Buddhists and even Hindus, old as these faiths are. In the Stone Age, humankind's time on the one hand, and the domestic pursuits of agriculture, home making, medicine and maintaining the fire in the hearth on the other. The hunting, fishing and fighting was the job of the man, the rest the domain of woman. Life was possible only if one came to terms with the forces of nature, be they terrible or friendly, and so these forces were worshipped as deities by the simple people of the Stone Age.

Presiding over all hunting activities was of course the Horned God of the hunt. Men would impersonate this deity by wearing animal skins and horns in dance rituals called sympathetic magic, based on the belief that dressing the part makes one into the character one represents. From this costume, the medieval Christian Church thousands of years later constructed the image of the horned devil.

Woman, on the other hand, had the dual task of propagating the race through fertility and maintaining the home as guardian of the fire, so the Mother Goddess of all creation naturally was female, and because woman's place in primitive society was more important than man's, the old Horned God became subordinated to the image of the Mother Goddess.

In worshipping the sun, the Stone Age people thought of the male god of the hunt while the moon, the night, and all the mysteries of life were associated with the Mother Goddess.

Every civilization had a religion of this kind: in Western Europe it was simply the Horned God and the Mother Goddess; in Greece, Pan and Diana; and in Asia, Cybele and Atys.

As time went on, the priestess of the Mother Goddess added medicine and a knowledge of nature's herbs to her storehouse of knowledge; and since the question of life and death was always present in primitive society, the raising of the dead also mattered and again the priestess was in charge. Only during the winter season, when the hunter was in his element, did the male priest preside at the religious gatherings, and primarily in a ceremonial function. Thus Witchcraft, the religion of the Stone Age, was essentially matriarchal.

The Old Religion, as it was called when Christianity appeared upon the scene, coexisted at first peacefully with the new faith. In fact, early Christianity borrowed much from the older religion, incorporating native customs, raising churches upon sacred pagan sites, and allowing the country people to continue going to the witchcraft gatherings, the sabbats and the esbats, so long as they also came to church on Sunday.

But by the seventh century, Christianity had become a fanatical religion and the continued influence of another religion side by side with the Church became troublesome. Added to this was the beginning intellectual development of early reform movements. By the tenth century, such sects as the Albigensi and Waldensi had risen and were ruthlessly exterminated by the Roman Church. Gradually the Old Religion felt the climate change and went underground, but despite decline in the number of its people, there was a continuance of worship in Western Europe all the way from the

Stone Age to the present. The Church had turned all the gods of the pagans into demons, and every evil in the world, every disease, quite naturally was the work of some specific demon who had to be discovered and then destroyed. As yet, the devil had not been born. The peasant riot of 1364 showed the Church how dangerous could be the *organized* discontent of the underprivileged masses, and a scapegoat had to be found quickly. It was then that some church theoreticians thought of creating a central figure who would be the feared Antichrist; the counter-player whose presence in this world was the cause of all evil, and who, conversely, was kept in power only because of the sins committed by some humans. At the head of the list of such sins was the sin of not accepting Church dogma and Jesus Christ as the son of God. The practitioners of the Old Religion, having worshipped their way without Jesus for so long, quite naturally saw no reason to submit to such—to them—alien philosophy. But the Church was not satisfied with the figure of a vague Antichrist; he took the identity of the horned devil, conjured up from a mixture of the ancient Phoenician Beelzebub, and Pan, plus the fertile imagination of a sexually and intellectually frustrated clergy who were forbidden any form of discussion or even constructive thinking outside Catholic doctrine. Torture, punishment for one's sins and physical suffering were part of medieval thinking and so the devil visited all those things upon the poor soul he managed to snatch. Witches, the Church asserted, had a compact with the devil and therefore were had a compact with the devil and therefore were his associates. By 1485, the Pope had been persuaded to actively persecute them *en masse,* and from then on literally millions of people died innocently in the most horrible ways. The two great waves of witch hunting from the 15th to the 17th century, and again in the late 17th, when the Puritans equalled their Roman Catholic brethren in ferocity, were a carnival of death sparing neither high nor low: accusation of witchcraft was tantamount to conviction, and many were caught up in this madness simply because a neighbor wanted their property badly enough to accuse them before the authorities.

The belief in the devil was so universal, that anyone stating he *didn't,* would automatically convict *himself!*

Witches do not believe in the devil, but a happy life free of sin and culminating in death followed by reincarnation. In their religion there simply is no place for so sinister a figure as Satan.

The accused witches were inevitably forced to confess to the weirdest of doings, which, under torture, they readily enough did. Riding through the air on broomsticks for instance, which the Church Inquisitors thought witches did habitually, was actually a misinterpretation of two separate and very real customs. At the gatherings of the country folk, the women would bring their brooms as symbols of domestic virtue. They would then ride around the circle astride these brooms ceremoniously, after which they would jump a few times with their brooms, to "show the grain how high to grow."

Whenever Witches could not attend a nocturnal rite, they would anoint themselves with a hallucinogenic salve made from nightshade, belladonna and other delusion-producing herbs. Although their imaginations soared high, and their fantasies were fierce, these Witches actually never left their beds.

Nor do Witches ever practice the Black Mass, a blasphemous mockery of the real Mass. Since Witches do not accept Christianity in the first place, it stands to reason they would not waste their time mocking something they don't believe in.

To be sure, some people have performed Black Masses, mainly from the Renaissance period onward, but they were thrill seekers, depraved, unbalanced people, and certainly not Witches.

Due to the persecutions, Witchcraft, especially in Europe, went completely underground and only the so-called hereditary witches continued to practice their ancient faith in private, ever fearful of being found out.

By the dawn of the 19th century, the age of reason had also dawned in respect to witchcraft persecutions and they were left alone. But so deeply had the Church left her mark upon these unfortunate people, that freedom from persecution did not automatically encourage their return to the light. It was not until 1951, when the ancient witchcraft rite was finally repudiated in Britain, that the Craft established itself once again witchcraft families that had survived all those centuries of persecution, were not exactly eager to invite strangers to their rituals or go on television.

In America a sudden spurt of witchcraft persecutions in the 1690's had its origin in a comparatively minor and unconnected event: the West Indian servant girl of one of Salem's citizens, a Puritan, came out with psychic experiences, including trance mediumship. To the superstitious and untrained Puritans, this sounded like the work of the devil. The girl was pressured into admitting having had a compact with the Prince of Darkness and, faced with mortal danger, decided to pull a few respectable ladies of the community down with her. Before long, the hysteria had spread all over Salem, dozens of people were in jail or on trial as witchcraft practitioners in league with Satan and the very people who had come to America to escape persecution for their religious beliefs sat in judgment over them.

By comparison with European holocausts, the number of victims at Salem was small, but the stench of their death will never quite drift away from the sleepy little New England town. Centuries later, every one of the accused was exonerated by a court of inquiry.

Even today there are sporadic outbursts of intolerance, especially in remote areas or small towns, where Bible-conscious people feel hot under the collar when they hear of fellow Americans practicing Witchcraft. But it is mainly a lack of understanding and communication. Witches don't invite outsiders, they truly practice their ancient law of "An it harm none, do what thou wilt," and they couldn't care less what others believe or don't believe. I think they're entitled to the same respect.

As I write these lines, I look forward to a nationwide "Gathering of the Tribes" in the northern Georgia mountains. I look forward to meeting some new Witches, and some old ones I haven't talked to in—ah—a spell: "old" of course only in terms of my knowing them, for Witches, somehow, seem to be forever young. Maybe it's because they're at peace with nature, and thus with themselves?

# WHEN UFOs LAND: PHYSICAL EVIDENCE vs. CULTISTS

## *(The Ufonauts)*

The main purpose of the present work is to come to terms with the reality of UFO crews, living creatures who pilot the strange craft from whatever world, rather than the far more numerous reports of sightings in the skies. But before I go into details concerning living people from flying saucers, I must state that I think the sightings are by no means explicable as weather balloons, stars, meteorites, and other so-called natural causes, nor do I think the landings involving living creatures are simply hallucinations which are better explained by psychiatrists rather than UFO researchers.

There may be some sightings due to errors of judgment, or reported by unstable individuals: there are bound to be some who like to get in on an interesting phenomenon. But I do not think that the percentage of deliberately false reports is any higher with UFO sightings than it is with any other observable phenomenon, that the number of unstable people involving themselves in such false reports is any higher than, say, people sending in false reports concerning a wanted murderer, or a missing person. If anything, the percentage should be smaller since the likelihood of being believed is far less in the case of UFOs than when reporting something reasonably familiar like a crime.

Over the last twenty years, I have been collecting reports concerning unusual sightings, without trying to evaluate either the reliability of the reports or their implications. Because one hears so often that UFO reports are the work of cranks or unqualified observers, it is perhaps wise to become once more aware of the quality of observers who have had *physical* evidence that UFOs are tangible, metallic machines, piloted by rational beings.

Mrs. Kathleen May of Flatwood, West Virginia, in the company of her two sons, aged thirteen and twelve, and three other boys about the same age, as well as a National Guardsman identified as Gene Lemon, aged seventeen, were present on the C. B. Fisher farm when they saw a ten-foot tall creature come towards them, frightening them. The creature was described as a "monster" exuding an overpowering odor which made them vomit for hours afterwards. The entity had a bright green body and a blood-red face, and bounced and floated toward them, rather than merely walking downhill. They had gone to the hill in the first place because the two May boys had seen a flying saucer land on the Fisher farm shortly before. The group had decided to investigate, and see for themselves whether there was anything to it. There was. Was it a monster they saw? Or did they simply see the occupant of a spacecraft, tall of stature, dressed in a cumbersome space suit, exuding a protective gas cover? This happened in September, 1952, and was reported all over the world.

Professional airline pilots make very good observers due to their training. Captain Francisco Rivas of the Venezuelan International Airways, was en route from Cuba to New York in October, 1952. He, his crew, and twenty of the thirty-three passengers aboard had occasion to observe an object outside their plane that was definitely not of terrestrial manufacture. "It seemed to have two exhaust pipes which threw off a bluish and yellowish light, like a fire," the pilot is quoted as saying. "It appeared about 45° above us and disappeared over the horizon three minutes later. That would have made its speed in the neighborhood of 2500 miles an hour." Needless to add, no manmade flying machines went that fast in 1952.

Two grizzled mining prospectors with a good record for sobriety, who withstood subsequent investigation by interested researchers, reported an encounter with people from a UFO. The two miners, John Q. Black and John Van Allen, saw the machine land on May 20, 1953. The machine came to rest on a sandbar in their remote area, a door opened, and a broad-shouldered small person got out, wearing what the miners called "a knee-length parka and Scotch tweed arms," scooped up a pail of water, passed it to someone inside the machine, and quickly went back inside himself after which the machine took off again. A month later, the same scene repeated itself and now the two miners decided to report the incident to the local sheriff, a Captain Fred Preston. They were advised to use extreme caution and under no circumstances shoot at the strange machine.

Private Jerome A. Scanlon was on guard duty at a Maryland Nike Base seventeen miles from Washington, D.C., when he observed an unidentified object moving very slowly about one hundred yards above his head. He observed that it was an aircraft of unknown design and had green and white trimmings but no markings or identification. "It skidded over the treetops, broke branches and then landed, sending up a shower of sparks and casting a weird glow over the whole area." Scanlon alerted his sergeant, Riney Farriss, and several other GIs and they rushed to the spot where the craft had landed. "By the time we got to the landing spot the craft was gone, but broken branches were strewn around and there was a scorched strip on the ground for half a mile." This happened in October, 1958.

U.S. Coast Guardsman Shell Alpert saw four large discs flying overhead in Salem, Massachusetts, in August, 1952. Fortunately he had his camera with him and quickly took a photograph. The picture clearly shows four round spinning discs, brightly lit, and not easily explained away as "natural cloud formation" or other such nonsense. No one doubted the Coast Guardsman's integrity, nor the authenticity of the pictures: but what had he photographed? Nothing of *this* world. Early in September, 1956, a farmer in Moneymore, Northern Ireland, by the name of Thomas Hutchinson, known for his sobriety and levelheadedness, described how he saw a small disc drop from the clouds into a bog two hundred yards from his front door. The object was "egg-shaped, about three feet high and eighteen inches in diameter, bright red with two dark red marks and three dark red stripes. It had a saucer-shaped base." Mr. Hutchinson kicked it over, but it returned to its original position. When he got down to his knees for a closer examination, the disc began to spin. He put a hammerlock on it and decided to take it to the nearest police station. Together with his wife, Hutchinson took the object and began to walk towards the village of Loup. When he got to a hedge, he put the object down for a moment to get his bearings. At that moment, the object rose of its own volition, and when Hutchinson tried to grab it, he was nearly pulled up with it. What had farmer Hutchinson found in his backyard? Perhaps he had come across one of the many little satellite discs reported, the kind of discs that are "spies in the skies" sent out by manned spacecrafts to report back information on conditions on the surface of earth. In this respect, the little discs seem to be similar in intention to our own satellites, and perhaps operate on similar remote control principles. But to the average farmer, it was an occasion to pray to God and ask for forgiveness for his sins.

A mysterious yellow disc hovered over London airport on March 6, 1959. The air traffic control officer saw it for several minutes through binoculars and checked with radar operators, only to find that no image was received on their screens! RAF Fighter Command got into the act next, and reported they had a "bright yellow light varying in intensity some 200 feet from the ground. It stayed in one position for about twenty minutes, then climbed away at high speed." A tangible object standing still in the sky for twenty minutes? Which does not appear on conventional radar screens? Impossible, unless of course, it was powered by an energy source different from anything known to us, such as antigravity or magnetic flows, and possessed of its own protective magnetic field, which would preclude it from being picked up by terrestrial radar.

United States astronaut John Glenn whose ability to evaluate aerial phenomena is at least as good as that of professional airline pilots, photographed a "mysterious object" outside his rocket, while on a space flight in 1962. The photograph clearly shows a flying saucer, with the cupola top plainly visible, and a second object, seen from a different angle, below it, or perhaps behind it. Nobody would accuse John Glenn of manufacturing this photograph, nor has anyone in an official position dared comment upon it in any definite terms. *Life* magazine has presented mysterious objects in the sky in a generally objective manner. In the issue dated May 17, 1963, *Life* presented a series of photographs taken a few minutes apart in such diverse places as Flagstaff, Arizona, then Prescott, then Phoenix, and finally Winslow, Arizona. The photographer is Dr. James McDonald, a meteorologist at the Institute of Atmospheric Physics in Tucson. According to Dr. McDonald, the "cloud" shown in the photographs is at least twenty-six miles high and thirty miles across, a lot higher and bigger than a cloud should be. Furthermore, the circle was too high to have been caused by a jet plane, and Dr. McDonald was able to determine that no rockets, rocket planes or bombs were being tested nearby that day. For the whitish, brightly lit cloud-like circle to be a genuine cloud is out of the question: no water droplets that could form such a cloud exist at a height of twenty-six miles. What remains is not just a mystery, but the possibility that the exhaust gases from a very large flying object, burning off in flight, were visible to the naked eye and the camera while the object itself, spinning at very high speed, might not have been, due to optical reasons, since objects spinning at very high speeds become invisible.

In still another issue of *Life* we find a report that "A Flying 'Something' Touches Down in Brazil." *Life* goes on to state that "James Pfeiffer, a respected aviation industry executive, saw and photographed a UFO while he was in Brazil. 'It was spheroid-shaped,' he reported, 'roughly seventy feet in diameter, very smooth in construction.' It hovered at about 1500 feet above the Lagoon Side Restaurant, where he sat, then sped away at 200 miles per hour and abruptly changed direction. Shortly afterwards, it set down in the woods across the water, emitting a high and then a low-pitched whining sound." The object in the photograph appears to be cone-shaped, like a spinning top, and there is a shadow area to the left suggesting that it was indeed a three-dimensional object—not a "hallucination."

The impact of this and other sightings was such that the United States Air Force finally decided to do some form of cosmic investigation, to let the world know that it was, after all, interested in the mystery of UFOs. That was when the ill-fated Project Blue Book, the Condon Report, was born. For the purpose of investigating what may well be the world's most exciting and significant subject, of tremendous impact to humanity's future, the U.S. Air Force put up a grant of exactly $300,000! This is roughly the equivalent of what it costs them to build half a small plane. One can readily see how sincere the entire investigation was from the very start.

But the United States was by no means alone in coming to concrete grips with "invaders" from other worlds. In France there had been a rash of reports, including some landings. Skid marks had been left on the grass, gashes on a wooden railway tie where the machine had landed, and physical evidence of landings made it plain that those Frenchmen who had had encounters with humanoids were not necessarily hallucinating.

Two bakers named Pierre Lucas and Serge Pochet of the village of Marcoing were approached by a small, bearded figure with one eye in the middle of his forehead. Gregoire Odut drew a picture of the "golden disc" he saw come in from the town of Wassy, and when it had landed, two small creatures came out of it, to look around. In a basketball court near Toulouse, a "dumpy little spaceman" was seen by a number of witnesses, including Francois Banero and Jean Olivier. It wore a spacesuit with large openings where the eyes usually are.

A professional meteorologist named Robert Rinker, on duty near Climax, Colorado, was taking a photograph of the lonely winter landscape which was his home at the time. When the film was developed, there appeared above his observatory a large, luminous disc, with a definite rim around it, evidently in rapid movement from right to left, with a sort of comet's tail behind it. The object must have been moving at very great speed, for Mr. Rinker had not seen anything with the naked eye.

Some of the photographs taken under scientifically correct conditions by reputable observers, and certainly genuine by any fair standard of evaluation, are exact duplicates of some photographs presented some years back by amateurs, such as George Adamski, whose efforts at the time were labeled outright forgeries, although no one really had any proof that they were.

It stands to reason that even advanced civilizations capable of sending research craft to our planet may at times make mistakes, and there are a few reports of UFOs *crashing* on earth. Elsewhere we have information that spaceships about to crash are destroyed by remote control from the mother ship, in order to prevent their remains from falling into human hands. This may well be true, because nearly nothing has been found in terms of crashed spaceships. There is, however, one persistent case which refuses to go away, although it has been labeled fraudulent many times, especially by people who do their research from remote libraries or in their own heads. This concerns the Aurora, Texas, case, going back to April, 1897. At that time the newspapers reported that a spaceship had collided with a windmill and exploded and that the pilot was buried in the town's cemetery. Aurora is a small town in north-central Texas, and the authorities there have recently discouraged all investigations, especially by amateurs who tend to upset the otherwise calm atmosphere of the little town. However, according to the *Associated Press*, of March 26, 1973, a team of competent researchers under the directorship of Hayden Hewes, director of the International UFO Bureau in Oklahoma City, Oklahoma, had been searching the abandoned, now weed-covered cemetery of Aurora for the spaceship pilot's grave. Old newspaper reports have it that the body of the pilot was dismembered when found. However, enough remains were picked up to determine that it was not the body of a human being. The body was then given a Christian burial in the local cemetery. The *Times-Herald*, a local newspaper, reported that a UFO had been sighted at 4 A.M. the day of the crash, and later collided with a windmill owned by a certain Judge A. S. Proctor. A U.S. Signal Services Officer stationed in Aurora at the time by the name of T. J. Weems, was quoted as stating the pilot carried papers with him which appeared to be a log of his travels, written in an unknown script. Pieces of the spaceship were scattered over the area and were taken as souvenirs by the curious. Both the cemetery and the remains of the windmill have been found by the recent search team, although it is not known whether the bones of the pilot have been identified.

Among non-scientific investigators of aerial phenomena that have thus far defied adequate scientific explanation is Allen H. Greenfield, of Atlanta, Georgia, who is a prolific questioner on the UFO phenomenon. Together with a group of like-minded individuals, he is responsible for a series of pamphlets called "Aerial Phenomena Perspectives," which later were expanded into what he calls *Ufology Notebooks*. These contain hard facts in the Fortean manner, leaving the guesswork to his readers. Mr. Greenfield, who edits the publications with the help of his wife Barbara, is an all-around occult investigation buff. A self-made man, he left school at the age of sixteen and took to the spiritual road. I asked him point-blank what he thought of the reality of extraterrestrial visitors on earth, seeing that he had access to a large amount of reports, and had had the time and opportunity to personally investigate many of them. Greenfield replied, "Considering all the data I have examined in the fifteen years I have been actively involved in UFO research work, I am very much inclined to think that there is a substantial core of validity in the reports of humanoid encounters. Nuclear physicist Stanton T. Friedman has presented a persuasive case for the possibility of UFO beings coming from an extraterrestrial, interstellar source. Making any assumptions regarding the motives of UFO occupants would be extremely difficult: we are sooner or later going to have to get used to the idea that alien beings may have truly alien thought patterns."

In November, 1968, a lady named Marjorie Holzman of the Department of Mathematics, Northwestern University, Evanston, Illinois, contacted me concerning some psychic dreams. It turned out that she was part of a small group of dedicated UFO researchers in the Chicago area, working for APRO, headquartered in Tucson, Arizona, but with subdivisions in various parts of the country. APRO is the brainchild of Mr. and Mrs. L. J. Lorenzen. Its membership includes many respectable scientists, such as Dr. Leo Sprinkle, assistant professor of psychology, University of Wyoming, Dr. Frank Salisbury, University of Utah, and Dr. Phillip Seff, professor of geology, University of Redlands, California. Their publication, the APRO *Bulletin*, is a respectable publication documenting what it reports.

An interesting incident which seems to have been ignored by American newspapers is reported by the APRO *Bulletin* of May-June, 1967. It concerns the observed landing of a UFO in Canada on May 20, 1967 in a wild area east of Winnipeg. The principal of the case was a Polish-born industrial mechanic named Steve Michalak, who was on a weekend prospecting expedition in the vicinity of Falcon Lake, seventy-five miles east of the city. Shortly after noon, he saw two red objects approaching him, one of which eventually came to rest on the ground while the other one took off again. Hidden from view, Michalak took a piece of paper from his pocket and began to sketch the strange object. He was able to observe it for nearly half an hour. He noticed that it radiated rainbow-like heat colors, but when it was airborne, it was more of a dull red hue. Half an hour after the object had landed, a door opened and Michalak was able to observe a purple light emanating from the inside of the craft. He put on his welding glasses to see better and noticed that there were flashing red, green, and blue lights inside the machine. At the same time, the mechanic heard a high-pitched whining sound as if a motor were being run at high speed, and he smelled a strange odor which reminded him of a burned out electrical appliance. Also the whoosh of air either being expelled or sucked in came to his attention.

"Michalak then approached the machine noticing the heat radiating from the object. He claims he heard the sound of voices, so he spoke to it, getting no answer." Then the motor noise stopped, he heard the voices again, then the door closed and the mechanic noted that it moved to become flush with the outside of the object, leaving absolutely no trace where the door had been. (Similar observations of rivetless openings in aircraft can be found in the reports of several other seemingly valid encounters.)

"Mr. Michalak then reached out and touched the machine, his canvas rubber-coated glove melting and slipping off the surface. As he looked down at the glove, the machine began to move in a counter-clockwise direction and he was blown to the left by a blast of hot air or exhaust which set his clothes afire." After the machine had taken off, Michalak managed to stagger back to his car and drive home. Immediately he felt dizzy and had to be treated at Misericordia Hospital for chest burns and his generally weak condition. He reported the incident to the Canadian Mounted Police but was given little credence. For several days after the incident, he could not eat properly and went back to the hospital where it was established that he had suffered from something akin to radiation sickness. "A curious characteristic of the burns on Michalak's chest was their arrangement in a checkerboard pattern. Some squares were marked with dots, others were not." Eventually, Mr. Michalak returned to the site of the landing with competent investigators from APRO, and soil samples were taken for further investigation.

One of the early reports concerning a UFO landing that impressed me very strongly appeared in *Fate* magazine in the early fifties, and possibly elsewhere as well. It concerned the experiences of a senior chemist at the Steep Rock Iron Mines, Ontario, Canada. He was having a quiet picnic at dusk on July 2, 1950 at the shore of a very secluded inlet known locally as Sawbill Bay. Suddenly, he and his wife felt the air vibrate, although no blasting was going on anywhere in the vicinity. Looking through a cleft in the rocks protecting them from view, they observed a large, shiny object resting on the water, looking somewhat like two saucers stuck together, one on top of the other. The top part had a kind of hatch cover which was now open. On the surface of the object they observed ten small figures, moving about like automatons, picking up a green-colored hose and drawing water from the bay, and discharging some other liquid into it. The figures appeared to be about four feet high, wore dark blue caps except for the one in the center, who directed the work; his cap was red. They were all dressed alike, had metallic chests, and darker legs. Within a few seconds, however, the figures disappeared into the hatch and the object rose several feet above the water. Then, with a terrific blast; it was gone from view.

I was equally impressed by the report of scoutmaster J. D. Des Vergiers, who saw a saucer land in a clearing in the woods near Lake Worth, Florida on August 19, 1952. Leaving his scouts behind him, he edged closer to investigate the strange craft and found himself standing directly below what he described as a dirty-colored disc about thirty feet in diameter, about three feet thick, hovering over the ground and spewing out some kind of exhaust. He was close enough to touch it, but the door opened or what he thought was a door, and he was shot in the face with some kind of weapon. He was later found semiconscious, suffering from severe burns. Strangely enough, however, the burns cleared up soon and left no ill effects.

I first read of this incident in the late 1950s. At that time it was particularly significant to me because I had just come back from the Poconos, in Pennsylvania, where I had spent some time at a local hotel called Mount Airy Lodge. One of the employees at the Lodge, aware of my interest in such matters, had approached me with a strange tale. He, too, had seen a flying saucer land in the woods. He, too, driven by natural curiosity, had approached the strange craft. But as he came close to the craft hovering just above the ground, his jacket and shirt burst into flames. Hastily he tore them off, and luckily suffered only minor burns. There were no ill effects beyond this, and he recovered quickly. His jacket and shirt, however, were a total loss.

Such concrete evidence by seemingly reputable people, supported by physical telltale marks, can scarcely be dismissed as fantasies. They are a far cry from such intellectual speculation as those expressed by T. G. Talmist concerning beings from outer space in an obscure esoteric journal called *Cosmos-Express*. Mr. Talmist argues that the star of Bethlehem might have been a flying saucer. He suggests that the miracle of Fatima was in fact a UFO landing, appearing to naive observers as a second sun. Talmist may have something in the latter case, although I have a different opinion concerning the star of Bethlehem as those who have read my *Star in the East* already know.

But even the most brilliant speculations cannot take the place of simple, factual observations and eyewitness reports. What are we to make of he is considered a major researcher in the field of telepathy. Dr. Schwarz points out that he has seen more than 3,770 patients over the past eighteen years at his consulting rooms, and yet not a single complaint involving a UFO sighting came from these many cases, proving to him that the subject was simply taboo, repressed and ignored. But Dr. Schwarz pointed out, "for many, UFOs are awesome and can tap the deepest wellsprings of emotion and become a highly personal or luminous experience. The accounts become tinged with cultural-religious factors, and, therefore, it is not unusual that some reports should have such trappings."

Dr. Schwarz visited me on December 6, 1974 to go over some of his experiences and evaluations of recent cases involving contactees and landings, especially those involving crews. He had become interested in UFO research in the 1960s. One of the first cases that caught his fancy was a landing reported on July 31, 1966 north of Erie, Pennsylvania. This case is known as the Presque Isle case, because it occurred at Presque Isle Peninsula Park. On this particularly hot day, four adults and two infants were on a picnic, having arrived by car. While the occupants were waiting in the car for one of their number to return from town, their car having gotten stuck in the sand, they suddenly saw a bright light shoot out of the skies, and land near Beach 7, about 300 yards from the car. Douglas J. Tibbetts, age eighteen, described the craft as hovering several hundred yards from the car, above ground, and Betty Jean Klem, age sixteen, described it as "mushroom-shaped with a narrow base rising to an oval structure having three lights on the back." There was a noise accompanying the phenomenon, somewhat like the noise in a telephone receiver, only louder. The young people were scared at first. The ship was large enough to come halfway up between the trees. Rays of light shone from the object and it lit up the entire woods along its path. Two policemen, Robert Loeb, Jr. and Ralph E. Clark, who had come along on a routine check, joined the occupants of the car in investigating the strange object. But after going only about 300 yards, they heard the stranded car's auto horn blaring frantically. Two women, Miss Klem and Mrs. Anita Haifley, age twenty, with her two young children, seemed terrified. When the men returned swiftly to the car, they were told that the women had seen a six-feet tall figure, apparently without neck or arms, in the nearby bushes. At the same time they had heard a scratching noise on the roof of the car. The car's doors and windows were locked, and the creature, whatever it was, did not gain entry. The following morning two policemen, Paul H. Wilson and Jay Robert Canfield, went to the area where the craft had supposedly landed and found strange markings in the sand, namely two triangularly shaped impressions about eight inches deep at the apex and then sloping upward to an area that was round and smooth. They found additional imprints leading to where the stalled car had been, about five to six feet apart. Later in the day similar imprints were found leading to the water of the nearby lake. The imprints seemed to have been made by what appeared to be some sort of claws. Plaster casts of the imprints were made by the State Police. A strange fluid was collected at the site, like water, but which would not seep quickly through the sand as water would. All those connected with the collecting of these samples and their analysis became violently ill shortly afterwards, although the illness subsequently disappeared. Dr. Schwarz concludes, "Although the objective reality of the alleged UFO accounts can neither be proved nor disproved, the data are entirely similar to many published experiences and seem to be authentic. The behavior of the participants during psychiatric studies was consonant with truthfulness for the reported experiences."

Another case which impressed Dr. Schwarz with the validity of such landings was published in *Flying Saucer Review*, probably the most reputable of magazines dealing with the subject, and printed in England. It involved the case of a flap of not less than seventy-nine documented "creature cases" in the Westmoreland County area, investigated by the Westmoreland County UFO Study Group under the direction of Stan Gordon.

On October 25, 1973, Mr. Gordon received a call from State Trooper Byrne that something unusual had happened on a farm not far from Greensburg, Pennsylvania. The initial witness, a farmer by the name of Stephen Pulaski, had noticed a bright light hovering about a field, and decided to investigate, along with at least fifteen other witnesses. He took his rifle and approached closer to where the bright red ball hovered over his field. The object was about 100 feet in diameter, dome-shaped, and made a sound like a lawnmower. As Mr. Pulaski and his neighbors were observing the phenomenon, one in the group yelled that there were two figures walking alongside. Mr. Pulaski immediately fired over the head of what he thought were the heads of two people, but when he looked closer he realized that the creatures were something strange indeed. One was about seven feet tall, the other, perhaps more than eight feet high. Since the fence posts were about six feet high, and the two figures walking alongside were higher than the fence, Mr. Pulaski was sure of his judgment. The larger creature's left hand touched and followed along the fence posts. Both creatures were completely covered with long dark grayish hair and had greenish, yellow eyes. Their arms hung down almost to the ground. The smaller of the two creatures took long strides as if trying to keep up with his larger companion. They were making whining sounds, almost like that of a baby crying, going back one to the other. There was also a strong odor present, reminiscent of burning rubber. The farmer then fired a second bullet over their heads, and when he saw the two creatures approaching his group, he panicked, and fired three rounds directly into the larger figure. "When the creature was hit, it made a whining sound and moved its right hand up towards the other creature, almost touching it, at which time the glowing lighted object just disappeared in the field and the noise from it also stopped. The creatures, after having been shot at, slowly turned around and walked back towards the woods." Even after the craft had left the ground and disappeared into the sky, the area where it had been was brightly lit, so much that one could read a newspaper by its light.

Dr. Schwarz was further impressed by the case involving one Gary Wilcox of Newark Valley, near Binghamton, New York. This farmer was out milking cows when he saw a UFO land, walked up to it and satisfied himself that it was a solid object. Two "little men" came from the craft and managed to carry on a conversation with the farmer. Now the strange thing is that these men from another world, allegedly, made certain predictions concerning our world. Even stranger, that the predictions actually came true. For instance, they predicted the death of an American astronaut, and shortly afterwards Astronaut Grissom did indeed die. "I spent a good part of an afternoon interviewing him," Dr. Schwarz reported. "He's probably a lot healthier than some of the fellows in New York with a clean bill of health." Wilcox described the strangers as being smaller than human beings and their voices coming to him by telepathy, as if emanating from the diaphragm. It all left him completely bewildered. Another case reported by Dr. Schwarz concerned Miss Frances Stichler, then age sixty-two, of Milford, Pennsylvania. Late in May of 1957, Miss Stichler saw a flying object no more than fifteen feet above the roof of her barn. "About fifty feet away and up about thirty-five feet from the ground, the saucer came to a stop in a somewhat tilted position and remained poised for nearly a minute." This gave Miss Stichler plenty of opportunity to observe it at close range. "The detailed observations which Miss Stichler made of the object are fascinating," Dr. Schwarz reports. "A man in a light gray, tight-fitting helmet and loose-fitting, shiny suit of the same color was sitting on the broad rim with his feet and legs in the lower portion of the saucer. The man sat on the rim on the far side of the saucer, facing directly toward Miss Stichler, the saucer being tilted so that his body could be seen down to his knees. The man, of average size, had deep-set eyes and a rather long face with a calm to quizzical expression. His skin was sun-tanned. The two looked at each other for the entire time. Then as the man continued to gaze at her, she began to feel disturbed and wondered what his next move might be and what she should do. About that time the whirring sound began to increase and the saucer took off."

Dr. Schwarz subjected the witness to his usual thorough psychiatric examination. In the end, he found her of above average intelligence and correct in all responses on formal testing in the mental status examination. In conversation, Miss Stichler recalled further that the occupant of the saucer looked like a slim, eighteen-year-old boy, had a uniform like a mechanic wears, the helmet over his head was to protect him and had no goggles, there was no hair showing, his face looked like that of a human, he had eyes and eyebrows, and hands like anyone else's hands with gloves on.

The case of Stella Lansing and her UFO photographs and movies also fascinated Dr. Schwarz. Mrs. Lansing of North Hampton, Massachusetts, had a number of experiences involving sightings in the early 1960s. Eventually she decided to take some photographs of the strange craft: later she used an amateur movie camera to film what to her appeared like fireballs moving through the landscape. When the film was examined, some of the frames showed three men, looking exactly like earthmen, in front of what appeared to be windows of some sort of craft. Dr. Schwarz says, "As an explanation for the movies, a hoax on Mrs. Lansing's part is most unlikely. My psychiatric studies of Mrs. Lansing show her to be an honest, intelligent, middle-aged woman who has had a profound interest in ufology for some time and who has had a series of unusual, presumed UFO-related experiences over the past several years."

Mrs. Lansing was accused of hallucinating UFOs, even committed to a hospital because of it. Dr. Schwarz spent years investigating her case, convinced that Mrs. Lansing was speaking the truth.

"Do you think the photographs are authentic?" I asked.

"There is no doubt in my mind that they are," Dr. Schwarz replied. "I have examined firsthand some of the most amazing reports of encounters with humanoids."

"Doctor," I said. "Are these physical persons?"

Dr. Schwarz thought this over for a moment

before he gave me his reply. "They appear to be and yet there are some that seem to disappear right before the observer's eyes. Also there are several kinds of visitors, all sizes, shapes, colors, from robots to various forms of life and creatures, tall, short, men, women; and as to where they come from, that is anyone's guess. My opinion is that the other-dimensional theory, which is now becoming increasingly popular, gives us the most fruitful area for exploration."

"Do these encounters happen mainly to people who are psychic?" I asked.

"Those I have studied do overlap," the doctor replied. "Many I know of are enormously gifted in this respect; haunted people, with poltergeist experiences."

"Do you know of any case where there has been a conversation other than by use of telepathy, that is, by direct vocal contact?"

"I think Stella Lansing heard things which she has recorded on tape. That hasn't been published yet. It sounded like tweety bird voices, somewhat like *dadadadade*. A high pitch, like a Morse code."

"Were they speaking English, and if so, was there anything peculiar about their English?"

"They were speaking English, and there was nothing peculiar about it."

"Could it have been synthesized speech?"

"Yes, sure."

Dr. Schwarz spoke of a contactee who had been telling some amazing incidents. I wondered whether his contactee was telling the truth. The doctor replied, "Yes, as he sees it." That wasn't good enough for me: either he was telling the objective truth, or not. Which was it?

"He is not making it up," the doctor replied emphatically. "It is something that was implanted in his mind, by an outside influence." Dr. Schwarz refused to give me the man's name, except to say that his first name was John, that he was a retired man now living in the South. The man, a retired engineer and inventor, got his contacts inside his head so to speak, and they told him to go to a certain place where a flying saucer would land. Sure enough, when he got to the deserted area in eastern Pennsylvania where he was told to go, a saucer landed and a humanoid got out to talk to him—in German! John was then taken aboard and shown the inside of the flying saucer, because he was an inventor, after all. But unlike other cases, John was allowed to remember what he had seen, and even better, tell his psychiatrist, Dr. Schwarz.

I wondered, with his great interest in UFOs, why Dr. Schwarz himself had not yet been contacted by some reputable representative of the outer spaces. The doctor had no answer for that one, but didn't think that the extraterrestrials were about to land *en masse* in order to save humankind from itself.

"In your own mind, do you have doubts that machines from other worlds exist?" I asked him point-blank.

"There is no doubt in my mind that they do; however, we haven't yet exhausted the most fruitful hypotheses of psi. Still, machines are coming to earth from other places, but not in a way we understand machines: these can allegedly materialize and dematerialize at will."

Ted Bloecher, actor, writer, and serious researcher has been interested in the phenomena of UFOs since December, 1952, when he was fascinated by the famous radar sightings of UFOs in Washington, D.C. During the 1950s he became involved with a group called Civilian Saucer Intelligence, and later with NICAP of Washington, D.C., under the directorship of Major Keyhoe. Bloecher himself has not seen anything along flying saucer lines, but he is a very good investigator. "The last humanoid type case I was involved in was when I was a staff member of NICAP in the 1960s," he began. "I was a paid staff member. The case was down in Virginia, near Richmond. It was early in May, when a young student by the name of Michael Luckovich was driving home from a late date early in the morning. Rounding a back stretch of road he encountered three oddly glowing creatures in the middle of the road. Their heads were their most noticeable feature, because they were round and glowing, but Michael did not see any arms. It was all over quickly, because the three figures crossed the road in front of him and disappeared into a barley field. The next day he went back to check the field and found imprints in the soil. Unfortunately, by the time we got there, two or three weeks later, the barley had been cut and the traces were no longer visible to us."

Another valid case occurred in 1955 in and around the city of Cincinnati, Ohio. Leonard

Stringfield, local investigator, worked with Ted Bloecher on this case. On May 25, a certain short-order chef named Hunnicutt had a frightening experience in the Loveland area. He reported having encountered three creatures along the road on his way home from work. It happened around three o'clock in the morning on an isolated stretch of road outside a place called Branch Hill. He had stopped his car, thinking at first they were three "crazy guys" praying, because they seemed so short. But it turned out they were not kneeling in the grass, they were simply very short. They stood immobile at the side of the road. The first one had something in his hands that was creating an arc back and forth from one hand to the other. They seemed to have fire coming out of their hands. It may have been a signalling instrument of some sort. The three creatures were roughly humanoid, with a head on shoulders, and a rather unusual feature right between the shoulders and waist: they were described as being lopsided, the right arm longer than the left one as if to accommodate this unusual feature.

I suggested that this need not be a misshapen space traveler, but simply an individual wearing a spacesuit with various forms of equipment underneath, and Mr. Bloecher agreed that that was indeed possible. "The thing that threw him was that he couldn't distinguish any difference between the color of the face and the color of the uniform," Mr. Bloecher continued. "The figure was uniformly gray and there wasn't even a line of demarcation between neck or waist. The eyes were roughly normal; they were hairless but they had rolls of what appeared to be fat somewhat like the effect of a painted-on doll's head, although just gray in color. The nose was also more or less normal but the mouth was very unusual: it was just a straight line that crossed the lower portion of the jaw. The witness did not hear any sound, nor was there any telepathic communication. But when he got out of the car and stood there for perhaps two minutes, watching them, the figures turned slightly towards him and after several minutes he decided to approach them towards his right. The strangers, in turn, were approaching him from the left side of the car and when he got to the front fender of his car, they moved rather peculiarly toward him not as if they were actually walking, but more like drifting. At this point the witness felt it was unwise to go any closer, whether by suggestion or intuition is difficult to say. He decided to turn around and get back into his car, and drove straight to the home of the chief of police, John Fritz. In driving away, he passed the figures on the road, but there was no difficulty with his car, no electromagnetic effect of any kind, as is so often reported in incidents of this kind."

Mr. Bloecher began to investigate the case, but the witness could not tell him the exact date on which the encounter occurred. Bloecher was able to establish that the UFO sighting had been reported by a ground observer and the chief of police early on May 25, 1955. In this manner he was able to retrace the cook's steps and pin down the exact date of the encounter. Although Hunnicutt had not seen an actual UFO landing, he did sense a very strong and unusual odor, which he compared to a combination of almonds and alfalfa. Still another case occurred in roughly the same area which led Mr. Bloecher to assume that some sort of space investigation of the area was then in progress. The second case involved a civil defense volunteer driver who has insisted on keeping his name confidential, out of fear of being ridiculed for what he reported. One evening in July, 1955, he had returned to police headquarters as part of a routine check-in. That particular evening he was very much upset: he had encountered a group of foul-smelling small entities below a bridge in Loveland, Ohio. There were three or four small creatures underneath that bridge, and he smelled a peculiar, penetrating odor at the same time.

"Were there any other cases in the same area in 1955," I asked.

Ted Bloecher nodded. "There is a third case which involved a Cincinnati lady, although it did not happen in the Cincinnati area itself. She was driving with her husband through Georgia on the way to Florida, the date being July 3, 1955. When they drove through the town of Stockton, Georgia, not too far from the Florida state line, they encountered four short creatures on the highway. They wore a kind of hooded cape, and one of them was standing in her lane, facing the car, so she got a fairly good view of him. The most outstanding features of the figure were the very large eyes which seemed luminous or reflective. She had to swerve in order not to hit the figure. Unfortunately, her husband was dozing in the back seat and did not see it. That summer, there was a fourth case in the Cincinnati area. This is the only multiple witness case I know of. Four teenagers claimed to have seen a 'green man' in Winton Woods on August 25, 1955. I would have written this off as a perpetrated hoax by the teenagers except there is no evidence to that effect, either."

"Have you yourself ever investigated a primary case?"

"A year and a half ago I investigated a case which originally occurred in November of 1964 at Harvey's Lake, Pennsylvania. The primary witness was a newly married girl of about twenty, first name Marianne, whose husband is a chemical engineer. For that reason she did not want her full name published. She had been spending Thanksgiving week at her parents-in-laws' house and her husband and father-in-law were off hunting in Canada for a few days, so she was keeping her mother-in-law company. It was late at night, shortly after midnight, and her mother-in-law had already retired. Marianne went outside to see what the weather looked like, and when she did she saw what she thought was a falling meteor toward the east, followed by a second one. Only the second one came straight down and *stopped*. To her it looked like a very bright light which slowly moved up a stream across the road from her house. The house is in a valley, with the stream across the road, and then there is a hillside going up a sloping farm, with a lot of underbrush toward the bottom of the hill, and the actual pastures on top of the hill. The object moved very slowly up the creek bed with a definite noise. Marianne called to her mother-in-law to join her, and she also saw the object. As they were watching it, the object returned downstream toward the house and hovered momentarily. It looked like a very bright light affixed to some sort of object, but they could not actually see the shape of it because of the brightness of the light. At this point it was only a few hundred feet away from them. It gradually moved up the stream bed and descended on the side of the hill, then landed in the pasture on top of the hill, which is roughly fourteen hundred feet from the house. Through binoculars Marianne and her mother-in-law watched throughout the night. For four hours the object stayed in view. They could clearly see a lot of activity around it. They saw five or six men dressed in what appeared to be black wet suits. The underside of the object was illuminated by a light and they could definitely see the curved under-portion of the object. The men had white faces, and they looked Caucasian. They appeared to be quite large, perhaps six to seven feet tall. The activity concerned some sort of repair work on the ship, as if they were taking out a unit and repairing it.

"Didn't they feel like going over to where this was taking place?" I asked, surprised at the lack of healthy curiosity on the part of the two women. Bloecher explained that the young woman was expecting a baby, that it was nighttime, and it would not have been easy to get through the heavy underbrush between the house and the bottom of the hill in the darkness. From time to time they went outside the house for a better look at the work going on, but eventually they returned inside the house, because it was a chilly November night. They decided against calling the police, fearing that this would bring on a horde of people with guns, and the idle curious. Whatever was happening on the hillside, both women felt it was not menacing to anyone, and it looked to them as if the individuals were very anxious to get something fixed and get on their way. For that reason, they decided to leave well enough alone.

Ted Bloecher is currently working with MUFON, the Mutual UFO Network, headquartered in Quincey, Illinois, under the direction of Walter Andrews, Jr. I asked Mr. Bloecher how much evidential material concerning crews of landed spaceships he had in his possession. "I have my own index, my own inventory of cases which runs close to 900," he replied. "This does not, of course, represent all firsthand material, but I have made a selection of about 150 cases on which I have individual folders, and a collection of what I call a reasonable assembly of firsthand data on the cases. So you can see, the reliable material concerning landings involving humanoids is quite respectable and voluminous."

"Are there certain parallels between these encounters?"

"There are very definitely prototypes in descriptive detail, as well as behavioral detail, but then there are also some wide divergencies. There are some of the strangest things which have been reported which make no sense whatever. For example, there is what is known as the bow-and-arrow case of September 4, 1964, in the Cisco Grove area of California. This was investigated by NICAP's chief investigator Paul Serni. The primary witness was out with two friends bow-and-arrow hunting during the first week of September, 1964. They got separated toward evening and the primary witness decided rather than try and find their camp in the dark and get lost, he would hole up for the night on a ridge. He picked a tree and secured himself in it, thinking that if there were any bears, he wouldn't be bothered. Since he was an outdoorsman, this was a customary procedure for him. Several hours after dark, he noticed a light on the ridge several miles away. It approached him and he noticed an object but could not really make out its shape. The object circled around the ridge where he had built a couple of fires, and he thought it was a helicopter. Then he noticed the object discharge a small object which landed in the undergrowth at the bottom of the ridge. Sometime thereafter he heard a thrashing sound in the undergrowth and eventually he saw several rather odd-looking creatures assemble around the base of his tree. He saw two humanoid creatures, hooded, with glasses over their eyes. Since it was already dark, he was not really able to see very clearly. In order to frighten the creatures off, he tore up parts of his camouflage suit and set fire to them, then threw the flaming pieces of cloth down at the two creatures. The strangers, in turn, tried to reach him in the tree and get him down.

Now there were two humanoids dressed in white, approximately five feet tall, trying to get up the trunk toward him. A second set of creatures that looked more like robots then appeared on the scene, emitting some sort of vapor from their mouths that knocked the primary witness out. He lost consciousness at this point and woke up the next morning, strapped to the tree, with most of his clothing ripped off."

I asked Ted Bloecher where in his opinion these strange creatures came from. Just as with most professional investigators of UFOs, he was very cagey with his answers. "From somewhere outside of our own frame of reference, on this planet, as we know it."

"Have you found any patterns among these contact cases that seem to indicate a purpose behind the landings?"

"Falling back on my own experience of sixteen years as an actor, I think that a lot of these close encounters, especially those involving occupants, have the stagiest qualities about them I've ever seen. What the witnesses are describing may be true, and they are telling the truth, but it doesn't mean necessarily that what they are describing is actually what is going on. Perhaps the occupants of the UFOs are doing "a piece of business" to test the witnesses' reactions. They may be doing a sociological study on earthmen."

"To your knowledge, has anyone ever been close enough to one of those machines to see the inside from the outside?"

"Yes; take the case of Mary Starr that both

NICAP and my own group in New York investigated back in December, 1957. Miss Starr was asleep that night in December when she was awakened by a bright light outside her window. Looking out, she saw an object hovering over her clothesline in the backyard. There were windows in the object and she could clearly see some short, humanoid creatures, at least three of them, through the windows. The object rocked back and forth over her backyard, and she was, as a matter of fact, above the object since her room was higher than the UFO's top.

"She described the men as having square heads and what appeared to be a light in the center of their heads. They were not humanoid, according to the witness, but had two arms and a kind of widespread body. She could not see the lower portions of their bodies through the window, however."

"Are you familiar with the so-called hollow earth theory? That the flying saucers actually come from a race living inside the globe?" I asked next.

"Nothing at all but a hollow-head source for it," Bloecher replied.

"In your book of about 900 references to encounters with humanoids, is the exchange of communication, when it takes place, telepathic or by voice?"

"It is often by voice and usually in the language of the witness. It sounds sometimes like a human voice, and sometimes it very definitely gives the feeling of a synthetic voice. In the Gary

Wilcox case, for example, the communication was in English but it did not come from any mouth but from a box or instrument on the chest of the creature."

# WHERE DO UFOs COME FROM AND WHY?

## *(The Ufonauts)*

"The universe is not ours alone," Walter Sullivan, Science Editor of the *New York Times* stated in a recent article in that publication. He continues with the rhetorical question, "Is someone trying to tell us something?" as he reproduces a characteristic pattern of the radio signals received from Pulsars, those mysterious outer space entities about which we know so very little. The article deals primarily with the possibility of signals from intelligent worlds beamed at us, and Sullivan, not a UFO buff, wonders, "have we finally begun to intercept the radio circuits that, some astronomers believe, may link supercivilizations within the Milky Way galaxy—the system of spiral star clouds that we inhabit?"

Why the signals should be restricted to "our" galaxy and not originate further out in space is difficult to fathom, unless Sullivan still thinks in terms of old-fashioned distance concepts. It wasn't until 1968 that these strange, seemingly "meaningful" radio signals were discovered by British astronomers. Since that time other observatories have set up machinery to intercept space signals, such as the observatory at Cornell University. It is at Cornell, of course, where Carl Sagan, the eminent astronomer, makes his headquarters. "The discovery has again brought to the fore the lurking suspicion that civilizations technologically far more advanced than ours may exist and that ultimately we may be able to communicate with them." Sullivan then traces the early attempts of humans to communicate with other worlds through visible signals on the globe's surface. However, these nineteenth and early twentieth century attempts at interstellar communication by people like Marconi and Tesla were directed primarily at the other planets in our solar system. At that time very little was known concerning these planets. Sullivan remarks that "the other planets of the solar system, including Mars, are now known to be so inhospitable to life forms even remotely resembling ourselves that the evolution of creatures as complex as *Homo sapiens* is highly unlikely."

While he dismisses the probability of any kind of humanoid life within our solar system, Sullivan points out that there are roughly 150 billion stars in the Milky Way galaxy alone, not to mention other galaxies. "Through various lines of scientific reasoning it has been concluded that a certain percentage of these stars must have planets in orbit around them, and of these some must resemble the earth in all those respects necessary for the evolution of life."

Quite so, but as yet we are not altogether sure whether the planets of our own system may not harbor at the very least some bases for aliens to use as way stations toward earth. Whether indigenous life exists in the solar system is debatable, and the odds at present seem against it, but certainty does not exist as yet.

Sullivan points out that these distant galaxies are millions and billions of light years away from us, and that even one light year is an enormous distance to travel. "It is therefore doubtful that, using either light or radio signals, we could ever communicate with life in another spiral galaxy." He concedes that within our own galaxy there are several sunlike stars closer than thirty light years, and that an exchange of signals between us and them is indeed a possibility.

The Scottish scientist, Duncan Lunan, believes he received and translated a message sent to earth by a robot spacecraft from a highly advanced civilization beyond our system. According to Lunan, this automated vehicle may have been circling the moon for thousands of years waiting patiently for people on earth to acquire the necessary knowledge on how to contact it. According to Dr. Ronald N. Bracewell of Stanford University, a much more advanced civilization than ours might "build large numbers of automated messengers to probe other planetary systems. Such vehicles would carry computers comparable in their ability to the human brain. Each would be designed to orbit the star to which it was assigned until it heard narrow band radio signals such as those that might be generated by a civilization entering upon its technological stage." Dr. Bracewell, according to the *New York Times*, then concludes that we ought to be on the lookout for signals from such a messenger, "in our own solar system."

Lunan, who wrote of his amazing discovery in *Interstellar Contact*, reported that he had stumbled upon a kind of SOS message sent from a point in the constellation Böotis some thirteen thousand years ago, from a planet long considered uninhabitable. He theorizes that this is a signal from a civilization in search for another home prior to its own planet being burned up in the heat of its expanding sun. Lunan deciphered the communication as follows:

"Our home is Epsilon Böotis, which is a double star. We live on the sixth planet of seven counting outwards from the sun, which is the larger of the two stars. Our sixth planet has one moon. Our fourth planet has three. Our first and third planets each have one. Our probe is in the orbit of your moon." Duncan Lunan's discovery caused a major controversy, in view of Lunan's eminent position as a reputable scientist. His theories have been supported by the accounts of Russian scientists concerning similar signals from space. Lunan, of course, did not get the message from Epsilon Böotis like a Western Union message; the seemingly organized radio signal had to be analyzed, and with the help of complicated graphs, Lunan was able to turn the dots he had received into intelligible "messages."

There are three requirements for life as we

know it to exist outside our own world: a sun of the proper warmth and longevity; a planet large enough to retain an oxygen atmosphere and yet small enough to allow its hydrogen to escape into space; and a temperature on the surface of the planet at which water remains a liquid. As far as life as we do *not* know it, is concerned, indications point to the existence of parallel life forms in space, and no hard evidence exists for bizarre forms of life that could sustain themselves without a proper atmosphere or the other two conditions.

Concerning the origin of the Ufonauts, Dr. Harold C. Urey, atomic scientist and Nobel prize winner, stated, "Mars alone shows evidence of some low form of plant life. We believe other planets in our solar system are largely desert and waterless." He did not think that our solar system was the point of origin for the UFOs. But Dr. Hermann Oberth, "the father of the German rocket program," later working on American guided missiles, said, "I am confident that they do not originate in our solar system but use Mars or some other body as a way station." Dr. E. C. Slipher, of Lowell Observatory observed, during the so-called Operation Mars in the summer of 1953, that UFO sightings increased greatly whenever Mars was at its closest approach to earth.

Of course, belief that life exists in space is not a new idea by a long shot. Giordano Bruno claimed that "there are innumerable suns and innumerable earths which revolve around their suns, as our seven planets revolve around our sun ... worlds inhabited by living creatures." He was jailed for his heretic beliefs, and burned at the stake in 1600 A.D. Some eighty years later, the Copernican system, which stated that the earth revolves around the sun, gained general recognition, and the possibility of life in space was again mentioned.

One of the problems found insurmountable by otherwise very imaginative researchers is the problem of distances and the time it would take entities from space to reach our system. According to Dr. J. E. Lipp, working for the U.S. Air Force's Project Sign, "conceivably, among the myriads of stellar systems in the galaxy, one or more races have discovered methods of travel that would be fantastic by our standards."

John Keel states, "Ideas which have been accepted fact for many years have suddenly been proved completely false ... space probes to Mars and Venus have tossed innumerable astronomical theories into a cocked hat. Recent radar probes to the planet Mercury discovered that that planet is actually rotating slowly on its axis, even though millions of school children have been taught for generations that Mercury does *not* rotate ... Before the end of this century all the textbooks will have to be scrapped."

Several years ago, University of Maryland physicist Joseph Weber discovered gravitation waves from somewhere in space. According to Weber, they represented the first evidence of gravitational fields in action, much like pressure waves in the air that are the carriers of sound waves. Weber considered his findings a confirmation of one of Albert Einstein's unproven theories concerning the possible harnessing of gravitational energy. "There is a hundred times as much gravity energy in the universe as nuclear energy," Weber said

Despite many significant incidents and much research going on in the field, the point of origin for the space vehicles remained a subject for discussion rather than solid fact. It wasn't until the "interrupted journey" of Barney and Betty Hill in 1961 that a breakthrough came that allows us to pinpoint at least one point of origin for extraterrestrial vehicles and visitors. Although the discovery of the "star map" occurred several years ago, it has not been publicized outside the immediate field of UFO research. In an interview given to the *Springfield Daily News,* Betty Hill made a first announcement concerning the study undertaken by astronomer Marjorie E. Fish of Ohio concerning the validity of the star map Betty Hill had sketched from memory. Marjorie Fish spent six years validating that drawing. Actually, the map was drawn three years after the abduction itself, when the Hills worked with Dr. Simon, and through hypnotherapy regained a stronger memory of what they had experienced aboard the UFO. During my visit to Betty Hill at her mother's house in New Hampshire I asked her to put into her own words what the star map looked like.

"They showed me a three-dimensional map, it was sort of in the wall in a way. The leader explained what the lines from one to the other round ball meant—heavy lines were trade routes, where they went all the time, lighter lines were places they went to occasionally, and broken lines were expeditions." (However, as Betty Hill was unable to show the leader where earth was on his map, he refused to tell her where they had come from.) Unfortunately there were no names to the stars on the map, and to Betty it was like "looking out a window."

"He also said that our sun was on the map, but I didn't know at that time where it was," Betty added, when I spoke to her again about this on a second occasion, November 12, 1974. "There were twelve stars on the map, and they were luminous, like round balls suspended with light shining from somewhere onto them."

After the star map had been drawn, Betty Hill had no idea what it signified. When it was announced that Russian astronomers had picked up radio signals from the constellation Pegasus, Betty Hill compared her diagram with that published by the Russians and found certain similarities. But not being an astronomer, her guess was at best an educated guess. It turned out, thanks to Marjorie Fish, that the map did not represent the constellation Pegasus, after all. But teacher and amateur astronomer Marjorie Fish had a new idea: that the star map was drawn, not from our terrestrial viewpoint, but from that of the Ufonauts! Miss Fish began to build models with the sun in the center, each model a number of light years out; until she reached sixty-five light years out, and eventually she turned this into a model containing all the stars in that part of our galaxy.

"There was no other pattern of stars in the sky that resembled in any way my star map but this one pattern," Betty Hill explained. The map drawn from memory by Betty Hill appeared to be a section map, possibly pulled out to navigate by since the airship was then within the confines of that map. The sector shown to Betty Hill by the captain was approximately forty-eight light-years across and thirty-six in width. With that area there are up to 200 stars, but according to studies undertaken by astronomers and exobiologists, there are only twelve stars with characteristics capable of having planets that would support some form of life. "And out of those hundreds of stars, I picked those twelve," Betty said with a quiet display of pride. She had, of course, no knowledge of the heavens, nor why these twelve stars had any meaning.

These twelve stars are called "main sequence stars" by astronomers, meaning that they have developed over a certain number of years and become stable, and are thus capable of supporting planets. By this form of reckoning, earth is at the beginning stage of life development, and the home base of Betty Hill's Ufonauts is a much older planet, thus more technologically advanced.

The star map that led authors Stanton Friedman and B. Ann Slate to declare "UFO star base discovered" in an article in *Saga* magazine, July, 1973, shows our sun in the upper right corner, with the two double stars Zeta Reticuli 1 immediately below and below it, to the right, Zeta Reticuli 2. A double line connects our sun with Zeta

Reticuli 1, while the two dual suns are connected by quadruple lines, thus indicating, if the captain's explanation is applied, a lively shuttle traffic between the two halves of this particular star system. Apparently, the Ufonauts also visited 82 Eridani and Zeta Tucanae frequently, judging from the double lines connecting them with the base at Zeta Reticuli 1. This would indicate life on planets around those two suns as well, while the broken double line continuing the path from 82 Eridani to Tau Ceti indicated expeditions. Single broken lines connect Tau Ceti onward with 107 Piscium, then onto 54 Piscium, and up to Gliese 67. Another thrust continues from Zeta Tucanae to Tau Eridani and separately to Cet 1. This makes it a total of twelve stars, outside our sun. In addition, Betty Hill's map also shows three stars between Tau Eridani and Cet 1 that the Ufonauts apparently did not travel to at all, and the sun Formalhaut between Zeta Tucanae and Tau Ceti, also without a connecting link to any of the other suns visited. The Ufonauts must have had good reasons to omit these stars. After six years of "painstaking research and meticulous construction," as Friedman puts it, Marjorie Fish discovered the "precise angle of view and discovered that the Ufonauts were from the constellation Reticulum, some thirty-six light years away."

But *Saga* magazine, being a popular publication, was not likely to put the stamp of official approval on Marjorie Fish's amazing discovery, despite the superior skill of the two authors of the article. However, In December, 1974, *Astronomy*, which calls itself the world's most beautiful astronomy magazine but which is, in fact, a highly reputable magazine for professional astronomers, decided to present the case of the star map in a serious and painstakingly researched article by Terence Dickinson. In this article, which is complete with technical data, charts and professional jargon, likely to confuse the layman, the magazine supports the contention that thanks to Marjorie Fish we do know where *some* of the Ufonauts come from.

But rather than getting my information secondhand, I contacted Miss Fish in northern Ohio, and on January 17, 1975, flew out to meet her at the Toledo airport. A short time afterward we were able to sit down in a quiet room, with a scale model of her famous three-dimensional star map, and find out in detail how it all came about that we know some Ufonauts came from Zeta Reticuli.

Marjorie Fish had always been interested in astronomy, even as a child. Her father would take her and the other children out to discuss the stars in the heavens, and at a very young age she was already familiar with a number of constellations. Daughter of an attorney and teacher, she went to Juniata College in Huntingdon, Pennsylvania, and there she took the only course offered in astronomy. She was still only an astronomy buff, although a learned one, when her interest was drawn to the *Look* magazine articles concerning Barney and Betty Hill. "In fact, I didn't believe it at all when I first read it," Marjorie said, "but I also read *Anatomy of a Phenomenon* by Jacques Vallee, and revised my view concerning the subject of Ufonauts."

She then remembered the map that had appeared first in the *Look* article and thought that this was something that could be checked out. She decided to make this a major project in her life, and began to study all sorts of technical books on astronomy. But because she lived in a small town, Marjorie did not have easy access to the proper sources. Her professional interests veered toward biology, anthropology and psychology, but soon the quest for the identification of the star map took up nearly all her free time.

Marjorie Fish realized that the question of the parallax was behind Betty Hill's earlier opinion that her map represented the constellation Pegasus. "As you are moving through space you have a shift of the background and the constellations would not appear the same from another viewpoint as they would from earth," Miss Fish explained, "and looking at the map it seemed obvious to me that the base stars, the two large circles from which everything else radiated, were the point from which the map had been drawn. Since there were so few stars in that map and many other stars in the area seemed also suitable for life, I felt that the pattern had to be a very close one—why should they come to our solar system when they could come to stars just like our sun; why should they bypass equally good stars? The only thing we knew was that they had come here."

In eliminating stars that professional astronomers considered unlikely to have planets with life on them, Marjorie Fish eventually reduced the prospects to a small group of likely ones in two astronomical categories, those known as G category and some in the category K. By continually eliminating unlikely stars, eventually there emerged a pattern similar to that drawn by Betty Hill.

"When I was using all the stars, not just those likely to support planets with life, and there were over 250 separate components, the pattern did not emerge. You would think that out of that many points in space you could find something that was similar to the map. But it wasn't. This showed me the very narrow range they were choosing, much narrower than what I had started out with. I wanted life to be very widespread, I wanted them going even to the Red Dwarfs and the small Ks."

Zeta Reticuli 1 is the nearer of a pair of dual stars, very much like our sun. Unfortunately, our telescopes are not powerful enough to establish whether there are any planets revolving around it. Evidently the space people have better telescopes or other means to learn of our existence. "We can't even see a star beyond our own solar system with a planet the earth's size in our own galaxy, much less in some other galaxy," Marjorie Fish said.

"Do you believe that light years are absolutes or do they depend upon the point of observation?"

"Light years are just a linear distance; it is not really a time distance."

"Then is it possible that a person traveling through space might conceivably travel faster than the speed of light?"

"Modern physics would say no; I would say, let us wait and see. I would rather think there are things we don't know that maybe go beyond the speed of light."

According to physicist Stan Friedman, individuals in a spaceship could be covering the distance from Zeta Reticuli 1 to earth in about two years of our time when in fact they would be coming from thirty-seven light years away. But I do not think that the Ufonauts encountered by Barney and Betty Hill spent two full years getting here; their method of travel did not depend, in my estimation, on conventional means of transport but rather on travel by speeds far beyond anything we consider possible on earth. It seems unlikely that they would hurry Barney and Betty Hill into their UFO, saying that they had very little time, if they had spent two years reaching them.

I asked Marjorie Fish why the Ufonauts might have picked that particular section of the sky for their map. "There are several possibilities," Miss Fish replied. "Our sun is kind of in the boondocks, if you look at these other stars where they go, and it may be that they chose the area of our sun as the cut-off place. This was probably just a sector map, one of a great many maps they may have had. They had it displayed on the wall, because earth happened to be in this particular sector."

"What about the other stars marked on the map as places they visited regularly? Do they have any life?"

"Very likely; we only know their distance out,

and the fact that they are main sequence stars, which means that they are burning hydrogen at their most steady state. They are within the temperature range that would most likely support plants or life and they will last long enough for life. Of course, we have no way of telling how far along they are in the main sequence, so we don't know how far they are on the road into life. They are the kind of stars that could have terrestrial planets. I differ with some of the astronomers like Steve Dole concerning habitable planets for man. He thinks the planets around our sun have been distributed in a random fashion, and you could have a planet the size of Jupiter in the place of Mercury. I don't think so. If you take Jupiter and put it in Mercury's place, Jupiter's hydrogen atmosphere would quickly boil off and the more it would boil off, the smaller the planet would become. I think in planet formation the terrestrial planets are closer to the sun. My view is that the way planets revolve, there is a very good chance with three in the upper zone, Venus, Earth, and Mars, or four if you include the moon. Now it is quite possible that there may not be life on the two, but there could have been; they are not too far out of range to have had life."

After Marjorie Fish had constructed her model of the star map, she contacted Dr. Mitchell of Ohio State University, who had been instrumental in her research. She asked him to check it out through a computer, if possible. The thing that fascinated her was why the universe was not regularly constructed. For instance, on the edge of the area around our solar system, there isn't anything for about thirty light years out in one direction. But on the other side there are some very good prospects for life, one fourth of the area, while the other three-quarters promise nothing at all in that respect.

I reminded Marjorie Fish of Betty Hill's observation that the temperature aboard the spacecraft was considerably colder than on the outside. "Does this indicate anything about the nature of the home planet from which the Ufonauts come?"

"Not necessarily, because it may have to do with the area on their own planet where they came from, or perhaps their planet is slightly smaller or further out, but it has nothing to do with the size of the sun, more likely with the distance of the planet from it."

"Do you think that the great variety of reported appearances of humanoids indicate more than one point of origin?"

"Yes, there are twelve stars around the sun suitable to have plants or even life as we know it. That doesn't mean that they all do, but they could have. If each one develops its own life form you would have a very wide range."

Marjorie Fish is sure that her star map is exact to within half a light year; the distances between the stars on the map vary, from about one and a half light years to twenty light years.

"Is there anywhere else in the known universe a similar grouping like this?"

"This is not an isolated group; there may be more in the next sector map. What we have here is two-thirds of a cube. This would not normally happen if you were just taking a random group of stars. I can't even tilt the map a light year in one direction or another without cutting off some of the stars within the pattern."

"Is this then a deliberate map drawn to cover a definite area?"

"It would seem strange that they would make a round trip to the sun and not go beyond. That is why I think this is just one sector, and this star is their base. Of course, it might not be where they actually come from, it might be a colonized area, but it is definitely a very highly populated area. They have probably explored out in all these other directions, and since they show these as expeditions and not places they have solid lines to, and some of these are in about the same ratio of the earth, it probably means that the two Pisces stars are not suitable and they are not interested in them. They seem to go always to the nearest star that could have plants or life, and it is a very logical pattern. Now if you come straight up to Tau Ceti, the next closest is the sun, so perhaps on their first trip to Tau Ceti they would have used it as a jumping-off point to go to our sun.

"Now in our solar system they found something that interested them, so they had solid lines indicated on the map between their base and our sun, and they dropped the expedition line between Tau Ceti and our sun, just as they dropped the dotted lines between each of these other ones they have the solid lines to. But they did go to Tau Ceti as an expedition, so they have a dotted line there.

They have a dotted line also to 82 Eridani, so they may have used that as a jumping-off point, or used Tau Ceti again as a fuel stop or something of that nature. They stopped there again and then went on to the next planet with life which could be 107 Pisces or 54 Pisces. They must have been looking for planets that could have life. Now whether they are looking for colonization or simply for other forms of life, or other things, we don't know."

"What are they after on earth, what do you think?"

"Well, we've got liquid water which might interest them, because they've been seen over water quite often and seem to be pulling it up; we are the only planet in our solar system with liquid water with the possible exception of some holes on Mars, which, however, may be carbon dioxide."

"Why should they want water?"

"I suspect they are very similar to us in their chemistry, a carbon-based chemistry, and water is probably the solvent used for their life force as it is with us. They may be using it for industrial purposes too, and it should be remembered that earth is quite unusual in that it is made up of elements heavier than iron. The periodic table which I have here shows all elements, including man-made elements, in relation to each other as to their ability to take on other elements. We are the only planet in our solar system with those heavier elements, like gold, uranium, and so on. This might be interesting to them because we would be a source of metals like tungsten, gold, silver, mercury, etc. Even many of our common elements like zinc and copper are heavier than iron."

"What do you think is the metal used to construct their ships?"

"According to what was found in one explosion in South America reported by APRO, it is magnesium. It was a lot purer than our magnesium, but it was magnesium."

I asked Marjorie Fish whether she herself had ever had any experiences involving UFOs.

"I saw a number of things when I was living at Lakeside, Ohio. I also had one encounter which was fairly close, in February of 1969. A light was coming in low and Venus was on the opposite side of the sky, the moon was down, and it was a very calm and clear night. This amber-white light came over the hill where I was, and I judged it to be about four miles away. When I came below the hill there was what looked like some search lights circling around, and another little light was moving through the tree area. I ran over to get my brother-in-law and sister to see it, but they only saw it for a second. When I got to the area, there wasn't anything there."

Marjorie Fish would like to continue her unusual work, mapping still further sectors of the sky for possible sources of life. She has been unable to get an official grant of any sort, but eventually took a job as health physics technician at Oak Ridge National Laboratory in Tennessee, where she is now.

There was still another interesting element in the Betty Hill map, which seems to indicate its authenticity. Betty Hill saw the map in 1961, and drew it from memory, after hypnosis, in the spring of 1964. At that time it was not known as yet that Zeta Reticuli was a dual star. It was only in March, 1973, that the astronomer Van de Kamp discovered that Zeta Reticuli was in fact a double star!

*Astronomy* magazine shows the uncanny resemblance between the Hill map, the Fish interpretation, and the computer-generated map produced at Ohio State University as a check on the Fish model. The magazine also compared the sixteen stars in the stellar configuration discovered by Marjorie Fish (including those which had no lines connecting them with the base of the aliens) with the Betty Hill map. "If some of the star names on the Fish map sound familiar, they should. Ten of the sixteen stars are from the compact group that we selected earlier based on the most logical direction to pursue to conduct interstellar exploration from earth."

All the stars in the Hill map are solar-type stars, so apparently the Ufonauts weren't riding around aimlessly in space—they were looking for stars with planets most likely to have life, if indeed they did not know this prior to starting out on their journey. *Astronomy* also states that "both Zeta 1 and Zeta 2 are prime candidates for the search for life beyond earth. According to our current theories of planetary formation, they both should have a retinue of planets something like our solar system."

Another interesting sidelight is the fact that the Ufonauts avoided three stars that are shown on the map without lines, even dotted lines, and therefore of no interest to them. According to Dole, an astronomer specializing in stars most suitable for life, the three stars avoided by the Ufonauts are amongst those listed as "suitable for planets," but the Ufonauts evidently knew more than we do, and so they avoided them. Sure enough, long after the Betty Hill map had been drawn, new astronomical evidence (the Bright Star Catalogue) listed these three stars as "variables," meaning that they are totally unsuitable to support life. Also the star called Zeta Tucanae, considered one of those very suitable to support life, was not on the original Betty Hill map (it is, however, on the composite map, as it appears in *Saga* magazine). The reason for that is that it was blocked by the base stars: when Marjorie Fish eclipsed Zeta Tucanae by the two base stars, the map fell into place. This was still another test to verify what she had found.

"I speculated that they had actually started out for these two stars, but when they got just beyond a certain point they were able to see that these stars were just going on to the main sequence and so didn't have the planets settled down yet, or else they were variables. This must have been an expedition, so I suspect the reason they didn't have these in with dotted lines was that they weren't suitable and so they went on to another star. But again they didn't find what they wanted, because they didn't have a solid line here, and yet they have a solid line to earth, and a solid line means it is suitable."

"Are you saying the encounter with Betty

Hill took place on their way to those two stars, prior to their having made sure of their suitability, en route?"

"Yes, which probably indicates that they cannot tell if there are planets around stars which are suitable until they are actually there themselves or very close. In this case they were about two light years away."

"Wouldn't that indicate that their astronomy is not all that far ahead of ours?"

"Well, it indicates that there is probably no way of telling. You've got to know that there is a planet the right size, but also about atmosphere and so on, and you have to know how long it has been on the main sequence, how long a time it has had to develop. They may send out scout ships to find out."

Miss Fish then showed me some formidable charts, far beyond my layman's apprehension. Even though I have taken a great interest in astronomy ever since my student days, the mathematical aspects of astronomy have made it difficult for me to comprehend graphs and charts without adequate explanations. Miss Fish explained that smaller stars last longer than larger stars, because they do not burn up as fast and therefore allow the time required for life to form. Also, it was generally accepted by astronomers that slowly rotating stars were more likely to have planets than fast ones. The kind of star mentioned in Betty Hill's map belonged to a category known as Spectra type G. Our sun, for instance, is Spectra type G, number 2. The formation of life is dependent on even heat, and must extend over prolonged periods. Only the non-variable main sequence stars give even heat, therefore the majority of categories among stars known to us must be excluded from the possibility of supporting life. Even so, the amount of potential life-bearing worlds is very large.

As a result of the tremendous interest in the article dealing with Marjorie Fish's star map, *Astronomy* published another article in its May, 1975, issue, "The Search for Intelligence" by Ben Bova, in which the potential life-bearing worlds are discussed anew. In particular, Mr. Bova mentions what astronomers call dark companions, planets around a few of the nearest stars that are invisible but have been charted indirectly by the influences the planets exert upon their suns, due to gravity, causing the suns to deviate ever so slightly in their orbits over long periods of time. "Of the fifty-nine stars within seventeen light years of the sun, at least four are known to have dark companions and there are numerous suspected companions."

Clearly, Betty Hill and Marjorie Fish made a major breakthrough possible: no longer can serious astronomers shut their eyes before the evidence, even if they have second thoughts concerning the validity of humanoid landings.

I had hoped that during the private sitting between Betty Hill and Ethel Johnson Meyers the late Barney Hill might manifest through the trance medium. Afterwards, I confronted both ladies and asked them whether there was anything significant they could tell me. Barney had indeed manifested, at least to the satisfaction of his widow, and talked about many things, including a rather puzzling statement of an astronomical nature. The way Ethel recalled it, it was "it is Ceres, the goat, that drinks from the star at the tip of the Dipper" and it allegedly referred to the point of origin of the Ufonauts. According to Fred Hoyle's *Astronomy*, Ceres is a minor planet in our own solar system. Ceres was discovered in 1801 by the astronomer Piazzi, with an orbit of 27.7 of Bode's units, thus filling an expected gap between planets in our solar system. I am not enough of an expert to judge whether this planet from a certain angle appears to be "drinking" from the outermost star of the constellations called the Big or Little Dipper, but the puzzle bears further investigation. I then asked Betty to sum up what Barney had communicated to her concerning the nature of interstellar travelers.

"Some were good, and there were a few who were not so good; some had kidnapped people from this planet and taken them back. But most of them just contact people here and leave them behind."

"Something else," Ethel added, "they were trying to devise a new set of lungs, that they put the lungs of those they had kidnapped onto the lungs of their own type, which were not of the same atmosphere. Thus they could go from one place to another and live. In other words, the kidnapped people were given new lungs so that they could breathe the alien atmosphere. Also, that they were trying to grow lungs on their own kind, because of difficulty in breathing. Barney said we were lucky that we were not kidnapped and made guinea pigs; he made the comment that literally hundreds had been taken."

The question of strange disappearances of people has bothered some very serious researchers through the years. Brad Steiger, in a recent article in *Probe the Unknown*, discusses this disquieting phenomenon. He says, "Perhaps man is just another species in a vast game preserve, prey for some cosmic sportsman ... or do those who disappear accidentally stumble through some interdimensional door into oblivion ... "

He then goes on to list some hard facts, evidence for unexplained disappearances, not only of individuals, but of entire groups of people. He lists the case of twenty-year-old Richard Cowden and his son David who left the general store in Copper, Oregon, on September 1, 1974, after buying a quart of milk, and have not been seen since. Even his wife and their small daughter disappeared, yet their camping equipment was found set out, as if they had been swept up from the face of the earth in one single moment. They were never found again. People have disappeared from buses, from street corners, without rhyme or reason. What Steiger calls the strangest of all cases is the disappearance of an entire British regiment during World War I. This happened during the Gallipoli Campaign, in August, 1915. In this particular case, there is some fascinating testimony: various soldiers noticed "eight loaf-shaped clouds hovering over hill 60, located approximately three-fourths of a mile from the battlefront, in the otherwise cloudless sky." The clouds held their position in spite of the winds blowing from the south. From a nearby position, twenty-two soldiers watched several hundred men of the British First Fourth Norfolk Regiment march toward hill 60, when another loaf-shaped cloud, light grey in color and about 800 feet long, hung at ground level on the hill. The regiment marched into the cloud, dense enough to appear to be solid—and the soldiers never emerged from it. After an hour, the cloud rose gently, and moved northward. To this day, no trace has been found of the regiment, despite official investigations.

Dr. Berthold Schwarz, when asked his own view concerning these mysterious disappearances, conceded that there were what he called "windows" in many parts of our globe. He knew of a case in the Bahamas, where an alien craft landed several years ago. A local engineer walked up towards it, in full view of several people, and then just disappeared.

John Keel also speaks of special entrance gates, or windows, where spaceships can come in from distant worlds. These are supposed to be weak spots in the earth's etheric envelope through which beings from other space-time continuums can enter our world. Keel mentions Sussex County in England, the Mississippi Valley, the Ohio Valley, and some areas around Preston, Arizona, as areas of likely entry. Keel suggests that there may be a connection between high UFO activity and periods in time, and his calculations do show that a peak is reached on the twenty-fourth day of the month, and on Wednesdays.

Not all people disappeared forever. A Spanish soldier on guard in Manila, Philippines, on October 24, 1593, appeared twenty-four hours later in Mexico City. The case is documented and so is that of research scientist Paul MacGregor, who left his office in Boston to join his family on a camping trip, where they were vacationing. He never got there, but a month later walked into a police station in Buffalo, New York, with a case of amnesia. The number of such cases where people have no way to account for lost time is not inconsiderable. Keel reports the case of the young couple from Allentown, Pennsylvania, who were driving along a fairly deserted highway in July, 1966, when they saw a UFO overhead. It seemed as if it were going to land directly ahead of them, so the husband pulled the car to the side of the road and stopped. Then the object flew low over their car and disappeared. The husband started the car up again and drove to their destination, a summer cottage in the Poconos. When they looked at their watches, they discovered that it had taken them four hours to make a thirty minute drive. What had happened to them in the intervening three-and-a-half hours, they had no idea.

Sybil Leek was working on the case of a woman in the West who had been aboard a UFO, and as part of her experience had been taken up somewhere in California, only to find herself walking in the desert a thousand miles away minutes later. Still another of the many recorded cases reported here by John Keel concerns an Argentinian businessman who got into a new car in the city of Bahia Blanca when "a strange cloud seemed to envelop his vehicle. The next thing he knew he was standing alone on a deserted spot in the countryside." He stopped a passing truck and asked the driver to take him back to the city of Bahia Blanca, only to discover that he was a thousand kilometers away from it. In this case, the elapsed time had been only a few minutes. Keel also reports the case of Dr. Gerardo Vidal who was driving with his wife outside Bahia Blanca when their car was enveloped in a dense fog and they lost consciousness. When they came to, they were on a strange road, their watches had stopped, and their car seemed badly scorched. They soon discovered that they were in Mexico instead of Brazil, and that two days had passed since they had gotten into their car. The strange fog or cloud seems to be more than just a natural phenomenon: could it be that this is a device used by Ufonauts or some extraterrestrial agents to kidnap people? Shane Kurz, in one of the dreams she reported to me, expressed a great anxiety concerning just such a "cloud."

Which brings us to the greatest disappearing act of all, the Bermuda Triangle. Since the book of that name by Charles Berlitz was on the bestseller list for several months, I scarcely need go into details of that phenomenon, except to state that it is very real, despite some Johnny-come-lately detractors. Originally known as the Sargasso Sea, where ships simply disappeared, the Bermuda Triangle seems to be an area where a magnetic reversal exists. This phenomenon may be entirely natural, like a fault, although extraterrestrials may be using it for their own purposes. I rather imagine it to be a kind of corridor allowing them to come into our magnetic envelope easier than at other places. The evidence for the disappearance of individuals, entire ships, entire groups of airplanes and even large warships is documented and well-known. In one afternoon alone, December 5, 1945, twenty-seven men and six airplanes completely disappeared a few miles off the Florida coast and the search for debris never turned up any trace at all, not even an oil slick.

Ivan Sanderson, who made a study of the phenomenon, called the disappearing areas "vortices", and thought there were six of them around the world. George Hunt Williamson, in his book *Other Tongues—Other Flesh*, expresses his belief that people disappear due to natural magnetic reversions rather than kidnapping by space people. But that may be wishful thinking. Charles Berlitz speaks of "a door or window to another dimension in time or space through which extraterrestrials, sufficiently sophisticated scientifically, can penetrate at will ... Many of the disappearances, especially those concerning entire ships' crews, suggest raiding expeditions, ranging from collecting human beings for space zoos, for exhibits of different eras in planetary development, or for experimentation."

I have discussed this aspect of the Bermuda Triangle on several occasions with the author, and I have met his friend, Captain Don Henry, who is a surviving witness of an incident in which his ship was nearly gulped up by an unseen force. On at least one occasion a black shape was observed overhead, blotting out that portion of the sky and suggesting that some artificial object was hovering above the scene. Charles Berlitz's collaborator, the archaeologist and oceanographer, Dr. Manson Valentine, thinks that UFOs may be powered by atomic fusion rather than fission, which would account for the vortex-like tunnel observed by many people when UFOs are in flight. "Such fusion would build up a magnetic field which would power the UFO at incredible speeds and possibly bring into the same field other moving objects in the immediate vicinity."

Dr. Valentine speaks of several forms of propulsion used by the UFOs: in our atmosphere a perimeter of cathode ray generators would allow a disc-shaped ship to operate in any direction at great speed, allowing it to change direction at will and rapidly. The generators would ionize the air in front of the craft, creating a vacuum into which the craft would move. The other method of propulsion envisioned by Dr. Valentine would be a kind of jet propulsion nearly the speed of light. In this case the power would be furnished by atomic fusion and would be created from fusionable material and water—linking up with the many reported instances of a UFO seeking and taking up water on earth. There is also, in Dr. Valentine's opinion, a third possibility of movement into our dimension by dematerialization and rematerialization; in other words, by means of electromagnetic fields and quasi-instantaneously.

Ralph Blum in *Beyond Earth: Man's Contact with UFOs* observes that distance certainly is no problem to space travelers coming from Zeta Reticuli 1: if they travel at a speed nearly the speed of light, Albert Einstein's theory of time dilation would allow them to make the journey from a star system thirty-seven light years away in roughly twenty months. In this respect it is interesting to reread the amazing report of the Villa Santina case in which Professor R. L. Johannis, the witness, reports the departure of the space vehicle he observed at close quarters: "Meanwhile, the disc had tipped slightly away from its vertical position. Then it suddenly grew smaller and vanished. Immediately afterwards, I was struck by a tremendous blast of wind which rolled me over and over on the ground and filled my eyes with dust." Gordon Creighton, who reported the Villa Santina case for *The Humanoids*, rightfully points to the tremendous importance of this statement. He quotes a related case, that of Captain Howard, who had reported seeing a giant UFO over the Atlantic in 1954, which seemed to grow smaller while remaining at the same distance from the observers. Creighton feels that this is an indication of disappearance into another dimension, in other words, travel by methods other than fuel, atomic fission or fusion, or even magnetic fields.

I have purposefully refrained from mentioning a kind of space creature that may only exist in the fertile imagination of some writers, or then again, may have validity and represent an even more threatening aspect of alien intervention than the silver-suited crews of airborne UFOs. I am speaking of the so-called MIB, or "men in black," as John Keel has dubbed them, and of any human-type creatures who already inhabit our earth although from a different world. The concept of aliens being among us is not a new one; the Bible is full of references to strange beings coming from the skies; the folklore and religious traditions of many other civilizations have references to such unusual visitations, notably the traditions of the Mexican people, the Peruvian people, and even the Polynesian tribes. To primitive humans, the visitor from space had to be a god, and if he chose to remain among mortals or mate with them, that was his prerogative. But modern humans want to know who their neighbor is, if possible. So we have these strange and frequently bizarre cases of unusual beings startling the population, giving rise to the suspicion that not all beings are necessarily human.

"Could it be possible that normal-looking human beings are riding around in flying saucers," Mr. Keel asks rhetorically. He then continues that as far back as 1897 UFO occupants have been reported, looking just like people. But that we already know. What needs to be discussed here are Mr. Keel's men in black, who are not just like people, but seemingly *are* people, always dressed in black clothing, who turn up at the homes of witnesses to UFO sightings and arrive in conventional automobiles, not saucers. In many cases reported these strangers advise the witnesses to keep their mouths shut about what they have seen.

Cultists, aware of these reports, immediately assumed that they were dealing with representatives of the CIA, and it is true that there are instances when CIA operatives have advised against the disclosure of unusual encounters, such as a case in Brazil in which students had actually met Ufonauts and had been able to provide physical evidence by presenting metallic parts left behind on the scene.

There is the case of the Argentinian doctor, for instance, who was driving on a road near Cordoba the night of June 5, 1964, when he saw a flying object land in front of him. His car would not run any more and he decided to get out and investigate what had happened, when he saw a man approaching. The man asked him in Spanish what was the matter. After the doctor explained that his car wouldn't run, the stranger suggested he try it again; the doctor did, and the engine started up. As he put the car lights on he saw a UFO in front of him. The strange man who had spoken to him in his own language, smiled and said, "Don't be frightened. I have a mission to complete here on earth. My name is R. D., my friend, and you can tell mankind about it, in your own fashion." We already know that extraterrestrials can speak English, even if it is sometimes less than perfect; now we know that they can master Spanish, and we also know from Joao do Rio, a railroad worker, who was accosted by a UFO crewman twenty-eight inches high, that the aliens can master Portuguese. He, too, was authorized by the stranger to tell the world about his experience.

We are also indebted to Mr. Keel for the report concerning a certain Miss Connie Carpenter, of Middleport, Ohio. She had just gotten married and moved to a new address, and the phone had not been put in as yet. On February 22, 1967, at 8:15 A.M., she left the house to go to school. She was then just eighteen years old. As she walked down the street a black 1949 Buick pulled up alongside her and the driver opened the door, beckoning to her. Miss Carpenter thought he was asking for directions, so she approached him, and saw that he was a young, clean-cut man, about twenty-five years old, with neatly combed hair and a suntan, wearing a colorful shirt, and no jacket despite the bitter cold. She also noticed that the car appeared to be brand-new inside and out, even though it was an *old* model. What happened next is hard to believe. The driver grabbed her arm and tried to pull her into the car, but she broke away. The following day somebody pushed a note under her door, warning her, "Be careful, girl, I can get you yet." Sometime thereafter, Connie was awakened in the middle of the night by a sound that seemed like a loud beep, directing from outside her window. Needless to say, there was no apparent reason for these occurrences, and the stranger in the car was not known in the area.

In Point Pleasant, West Virginia, two residents were visited by "a mysterious couple who claimed to represent a firm which would take free annual photographs of their families, no strings attached." The two women described the couple as particularly odd-looking, the man very large, the woman with red hair, hiding her face as much as possible. No one else in the area received a visit from the couple, so there didn't seem to be any rhyme or reason to the proposition, unless, of course, the couple was a genuine pair of researchers from another world.

Perhaps the most telling account given by John Keel concerns a Mrs. Hyre who was working in the county courthouse at Athens, Ohio, early in January of 1967, when a little man entered her office. According to the witness he was about four feet six inches tall, had strange eyes covered by thick glasses, black, long hair and although it was twenty degrees outside he was wearing a short-sleeved blue shirt and blue trousers of thin material. Speaking to her in a low, halting voice, he asked for directions to a nearby town. As he spoke to her, he looked at her with hypnotic eyes, getting closer to her all the time. In fear, Mrs. Hyre got the circulation manager of the *Athens Messenger* to join her and engaged the strange visitor in conversation. At one point the visitor picked up a ballpoint pen and looked at it in amazement, as if he had never seen one before. On the spur of the moment, Mrs. Hyre gave him the pen, and he ran out into the night and disappeared. Several weeks after the incident, Mrs. Hyre saw the man again. When he noticed she was watching him, he ran for a large black car that seemed to be driven by a very large man.

All of this, of course, is circumstantial evidence. In another book, *UFOs—Operation Trojan Horse,* John Keel goes into great detail concerning the visits by aliens mimicking human beings, dropping in unexpectedly at the homes of some very ordinary folk; in fact, the people who were visited by these aliens were quite ordinary, of average status, and they represented a kind of unspoiled picture of contemporary lifestyles. Mr. Keel reports, "I have heard about strange men who paid pointless visits and sometimes posed as Air Force Officers. The descriptions are always the same—slight of stature, dark olive skins, sharp, pointed features. And most of the scattered witnesses specifically noticed that these men were dressed in clothes that seemed brand-new."

Whether the MIBs are figments of the imagination, government officials on business of their own, or authentic interference on the part of extraterrestrial agents, depends heavily on the quality of the witnesses. Since I have not been involved in any primary case myself, I withhold judgment, but I do not dismiss the possibility of such agents entirely. On the other hand, we must not be misled by the fantasies of a few UFO buffs who claim, usually through trance or automatic writing, to be in touch with intelligent worlds beyond our solar system, giving us fantastic details of life on those faraway planets, names of planets entirely from their own imagination, and on the whole a pitiful, psychotically tinged picture of what these extraterrestrial worlds certainly cannot be.

Like George Adamski, Howard Menger of New Jersey, the contactee who made the rounds of television and radio talk shows in the 1960s, claims to have been visited by handsome strangers from the planet Venus, appointing him a go-between for the people of earth. To dismiss Menger entirely as a fantasy would seem easy, and at the time when I first met him on a television show, I did just that. But on recollection, and when comparing some of his claims with similar claims put forward by later, perhaps more scientifically-oriented witnesses, it appears that Menger knew things he might not have known by himself, and that they might just possibly be true. His description of the space visitors, for instance, and the fact that they seemed to glide toward him rather than walk, meshes pretty well with a much more recent report, that of the Pascagoula incident. John Keel, who professes no belief in the extraterrestrial origin of UFOs but thinks they are from a different time and space continuum, a different dimension coexisting with ours here on earth, also considers the contactee a questionable source of information, and perhaps rightly so. Nevertheless, to dismiss *all* contactees as liars, as Frank Edwards has done, is dismissing a great deal of valuable material. When people like Dr. Andrija Puharich become contactees, one needs to look at the whole problem of extraterrestrial contacts with humans more cautiously.

But Keel has an interesting point to make: could it be that the contactees are telling the truth, but their informants are lying? And that they are lying deliberately as "part of the bewildering smoke screen which they have established to cover their real origin, purpose, and motivation."

As if it weren't enough to wonder about seemingly human agents trying to suppress information about UFOs and their occupants, we now have to worry about extraterrestrials doing some finagling of their own! As far as the Men in Black are concerned, a motion picture theatre booker by the name of Gray Barker wrote a book called *They Knew Too Much About Flying Saucers* a few years ago, and in it attempted to link the famous men in black suits to government secret service organizations. No less a responsible researcher than Ralph Blum wrote as recently as January, 1975 in *True* magazine that the U.S. government is by no means eager to disclose all it knows concerning strange visitations from extraterrestrial beings. In speaking of the famous Holloman Air Force Base incident, September, 1956, when a disc-shaped craft landed fifty yards from U.S. Highway 70 in plain view of dozens of commuter cars, including two Air Force colonels, two sergeants, and dozens of base employees, Mr. Blum reports that, after the Pentagon had been notified, "a flying squad of Air Force intelligence officers and CIA experts arrived from Washington. All base employees were assembled in a hangar, questioned, and sworn to absolute secrecy regarding the incident."

What exactly is the purpose of the Ufonauts coming here? Regardless of their point of origin, regardless of the diversity of appearance they undoubtedly represent, the aliens seem to have one thing in common: they are studying humans; they are collecting samples of our life; not necessarily people but plants and stones and artifacts; and they are very much concerned with what we do to ourselves in terms of destructiveness, especially of the atomic variety. It is a moot question why references to atomic destruction have not been received prior to the discovery of atom-splitting. Early reports of alien craft do not speak of such concern, not because atomic weaponry was then as yet unknown, but because the threat to the universe did not exist either. However, it has existed since the 1940s, and incidents of warning messages, advising humankind to stop atomic experiments for warlike purposes have shown up with increasing frequency. Nearly all the contactees claim that their "space brothers" preach peace and love and are very much concerned with our state of development, continuing warfare on this planet, and building ever greater means of destruction.

I asked John Fuller why he thought no official contact had been made between visiting aliens and people of substance here on earth.

"Hans, you are assuming a homocentric point of view," he replied. "How do we know we are not ants or beetles to them? Also, the Rand Corporation, I hear, has a twenty-five year projection of our space program in which they seriously consider contact with extraterrestrial planets. I understand they have issued recommendations that if any planet is encountered which seems to indicate an intelligent civilization through our space probes, that no contact should be made at first, but samples should be taken of the soil and the atmosphere, and not until a complete study and mapping of the planet had been done, should we make any actual contact. Also, if the aliens come intergalactic or interstellar distances, they couldn't bring an army that distance, so therefore they are unprotected and maybe want to find out surreptitiously; that is what it seemed like in the Hill case."

Dr. Daniel Fry, the scientist who reported his conversation with the absentee pilot of a spacecraft that had landed in front of him at the White Sands Proving Grounds, New Mexico, also wondered what the purpose of the visit was. "It is true that the purpose of the expedition is not entirely philanthropic," the alien pilot replied. "There are some materials upon your planet which we could use to the advantage of both our peoples, materials which you have in great abundance but which are rather scarce elsewhere in this solar system."

Notice Marjorie Fish's speculation that the visitors from Zeta Reticuli were after metals heavier than iron found in abundance on earth, but not necessarily in *their* world!

According to Dr. Daniel Fry, the visitors from space are trying to "help the people on earth alter their present flow of events and avert a holocaust which is otherwise inevitable." It appears, according to this informant, that the ancestors of these same space people, namely the races of Lemuria and Atlantis, had once destroyed each other on earth, resulting in a long period of decline for our planet. Now the space people do not want to see history repeat itself. Just like Andrija Puharich,

Fry was told to write a book. Just like Puharich, Fry was told that his communicators stayed in their spaceships way above the earth, able to control and monitor everything on our globe without ever having to come down to the surface of it. Just like Puharich, Dr. Fry was told that space people had chosen certain individuals to carry their message, to do their bidding. And again, as Dr. Puharich asked his space communicators why they wouldn't make an official landing and contact with people of importance on earth, so did Dr. Fry several years earlier under vastly different circumstances. "You must realize that any information which your government might acquire concerning us, our craft, our knowledge, would be considered the most vital military secret they have ever possessed," the Ufonauts explained. Puharich's informant also hesitated to let humankind and its leaders know too much, lest the power be abused. In other words, those of advanced civilizations do not trust us very much, and perhaps they're right. And interestingly, Fry as well as Puharich speak of a spiritual power behind it all, when one least expects it. "The spiritual and social sciences however, must come first. There can be no dependable development of a material science until you have first built a firm foundation of spiritual and social science," Dr. Fry's friend from space advised him. Puharich was told that behind all the strange goings-on, behind the power of the Spectra is the deity, and in one passage, he was told that the deity dwells within the tiniest atom as well.

But the lofty ideal of saving humankind from itself stands in sharp contrast to the minute, dispassionate research undertaken by so many of the visitors, who show an interest in human beings and our civilizations the way archaeologists show an interest in relics of the past. For instance, in the Betty Hill case, "the examiner said that he wished to do some tests to find out the basic differences between him and us." Barney Hill's artificial teeth disconcerted him, and the life span of human beings seemed to be beyond his comprehension, as much as Betty tried to explain it. Evidently, despite millennia of observation, the humanoids out there do not as yet know everything about us, although they know a lot. It seems that the contactee approach to space visitors usually includes concern for earth's welfare, and worry about atomic explosions: George Adamski quoted a "Master" as explaining the aliens were concerned with atomic warfare on earth because very large explosions of this kind could eventually penetrate earth's atmosphere into outer space and thus interfere with navigation between the planets of the solar system. This, of course, is predicated on the idea that Mr. Adamski's people came from planets in our own solar system. Adamski, too, spoke of God and a spiritual need sadly lacking in man today.

Putting aside for the moment the claims of contactees, and sticking to the hard-core evidence of alien visitors collecting samples of earth life, we find a large number of impressive cases, well attested to. Jacques Vallee is the source of the October 13, 1954 incident in Castelibranco, Portugal, where two witnesses saw "two individuals dressed in shiny clothes who emerged from a craft and gathered flowers, shrubs and twigs, then took off." In the same year, on November 4th, a Brazilian fisherman saw a luminous UFO land near the town of Pontal. "Three small men dressed in white, wearing caps of sorts, emerged from a door. They seemed to have dark skin, gathered leaves and grass, took some water in a tube, and the craft flew away." Gordon Creighton is the source of a report concerning a Brazilian of German ancestry named Rubem Hellwig, who twice encountered a small UFO in March, 1954, and managed to have a conversation with its occupants. "The crew were two men of slim build, about one meter sixty centimeters in height, their faces brownish and they were not wearing helmets. One was inside the machine and the other was collecting specimens of grass. They spoke to Hellwig in a strange language and yet somehow he says he understood what they asked, which was where they could get some ammonia. He directed them to a nearby town. With blue and yellow flames and great luminosity, the craft vanished silently and instantly." Coral Lorenzen reports the case of John Trasco of Everitts Town, New Jersey, who on November 6, 1957 went outside at dusk to feed his dog. He saw a brilliant UFO, egg-shaped, hovering in front of his barn. "He was confronted by a three-foot being with putty-colored face and large froglike eyes. Trasco said he thought he said, in broken English: 'We are peaceful people. We only want your dog.'" Mrs. Lorenzen also reports the case of Gary Wilcox of Tioga City, New York, which I mentioned earlier in my interview with Dr. Berthold Schwarz. Wilcox was visited by a UFO on the morning of April 24, 1964. The object had landed in a nearby field, and he decided to investigate. "He saw no door or hatch, but two small men approximately four feet tall suddenly arrived on the scene dressed in clothing which appeared to have no seams and a hood which covered their faces completely. Each was carrying a tray on which appeared to be soil removed from the field." After one of the men had informed Wilcox that they were from Mars, and he needn't be afraid of them, the conversation turned to the topic of organic fertilizers. Wilcox reports that he was questioned by the aliens concerning farming, and was told that the aliens were able to grow food in the atmosphere in their own environment. Whether the strangers were actually from the planet Mars or simply pretending to be from there, since that was what the population of earth would expect them to say, is a moot point. In the John Reeves incident of Brooksville, Florida, March 3, 1965, the Ufonauts also claimed to be from the planet Mars. If the strangers were doing this to mislead us as to their real point of origin, then I think their efforts were pointless; to an ordinary human being it makes little difference whether an alien dropping in from the sky comes "only" from the neighboring planet Mars or from a planet around a sun thirty-seven light years away. Perhaps the high command directing their effort felt differently—there is also some evidence that the aliens have tried to camouflage some of their ships to resemble more of our own ships, perhaps in order not to frighten us.

Coral Lorenzen mentions the case of Eddie Laxson, of Temple, Oklahoma, who saw a "fish-shaped silver object on Highway 70 near the Texas-Oklahoma state line. Laxson is an experienced electronics instructor at Shephard Air Base at Wichita Falls, Texas." When he investigated the strange object he saw a man dressed in what he took to be GI fatigues standing by the craft. He went back to his car to get a camera, but when he turned around the stranger was getting back into the object over a ladder and the craft took off immediately. Laxson could not identify the object, but he did get a good look at it. "The letters TL41, arranged vertically, were easily visible on the ship."

So where are they from? Venus? Mars? An unknown planet with a euphonic name like Clarion? Or are they from the further reaches of the universe, such as Zeta Reticuli, and places even further than that? Let us first examine the hard evidence in support of Ufonauts originating in our own solar system.

One of the best cases reported in responsible literature is that of police officer Herbert Schirmer and his encounter with a spaceship. As Ralph Blum tells it, Schirmer, under hypnosis, speaks of the spacemen he had encountered as coming from "a nearby galaxy. They had bases on Venus and some of the other planets in our galaxy." He goes even further to assert that "there are definitely bases in the United States. There is a base located beneath the ocean off the coast of Florida ... there is a base at the Polar Region ... there is another base right off the coast of Argentina. These bases are underground or underwater."

It is a fact that some sightings of UFOs include the plunging into the sea (without reappearance) of UFOs, and it is also a fact that many contactees claim that "their" people are from the planet Venus.

Dr. Jacques Vallee, in *Anatomy of a Phenomenon*, is by no means convinced that Mars or Venus must be ruled out as having life similar to ours. "The remarkable performance of Mariner II has not solved the many difficult questions concerning that planet, which is surrounded by a very dense atmosphere. Never has the soil of Venus been observed ... Mars is still very much a mystery ... it seems obvious that only space exploration, using automatic probes with special cameras, provides a means of solving the problem posed by that planet ..."

Do the UFOs originate within our own solar system? According to George Adamski and a few other contactees, they most certainly do. In fact, Adamski has us believe that there is a cozy interplay between men and women from Mars, Venus, Saturn and even Mercury who have dropped in on us at will, sometimes looking just like the people next door. On one occasion, Adamski reports an urge to go into Los Angeles and go to a certain hotel. In the lobby of this hotel he met the extraterrestrials who motioned him to follow and when their car was brought around, it turned out to be one of those four-door black sedans again, later made memorable by John Keel and his MIB. Adamski tells us that his conversations with the extraterrestrials were in plain English. "The speaker smiled and indicated to the driver. He is from the planet you call Mars. I am from the one called Saturn."

Dino Kraspedon (the *nom de plume* of a well-known Brazilian writer) is the author of a book called *My Contact with Flying Saucers*. In a way it resembles the work of Dr. Daniel Fry, as it details in sometimes quite technical language the inside and working mechanisms of UFOs. Mr. Kraspedon allegedly had his encounter with extraterrestrials in November, 1952. The parallel between the two books continues throughout both works. Both preach a gospel of spirituality and a turning away from atomic warfare. Both picture extraterrestrials as not having names in our sense of the term, and in the case of the Brazilian writer, we are told where the spaceship is from. "I come from a satellite of Jupiter." The captain of the UFO explained that he sometimes lived on Ganymede and sometimes on Jo.

The ubiquitous John Keel tells us of the strange case of Woodrow Derenberger, a simple man from Mineral Wells, West Virginia who made his living as a sewing machine salesman. One night in November, 1966, he saw a UFO land on the highway directly in front of him. As a result of this encounter, he met a man, about six feet tall, with dark complexion, and slightly elongated eyes, dressed in a dark coat and blue trousers that were quite shiny. There was some discussion during which Mr. Derenberger learned that the stranger's name was Cold or something that sounded like it and that he was from a country much less powerful than the United States. As with many other contactee cases, the UFO pilot didn't want to say too much at first but flew off, promising to return another time, which he did. Eventually he met some of the associates of the man he knew only as "Indrid Cold." They didn't always arrive in UFOs, to be sure, but in large limousines. Now the alien pilot told Mr. Derenberger that he came from a planet called Lanulos which was in the "galaxy of Ganymedes." Of course, Mr. Derenberger also claimed that he had been taken to that place and seen the large cities where the natives lived. It would be again easy to dismiss his story as a fantasy, but he was not the kind likely to have knowledge of a satellite of Jupiter named Ganymede.

Gordon Creighton, in *The Humanoids*, reports the bizarre case of another simple man, this one a Brazilian survey worker named José C. Higgins, of Sao Paulo, Brazil, who on July 23, 1947 observed a giant saucer land near him. There were several other workers near him who fled when the thing came to rest. Higgins stayed and saw three seven foot tall beings in "transparent suits covering head and body and inflated like rubber bags and with metal boxes on their backs." He noticed that they wore clothing underneath these coverings and that it resembled brightly colored paper; they had huge round eyes, large round bald heads, apparently no eyebrows or beards and their legs were longer than ours. Higgins found himself surrounded by these strange beings, and at one point one of them leveled a metal tube at him and it appeared to the worker that they meant to kidnap him. "At one point one of them had made eight holes in the ground with a stick and showed Higgins that the central one, larger (perhaps our sun) was 'Alamole' while the seventh and most distant hole was 'Orque' their home. This episode has been taken by some to indicate that they came from Uranus." Mr. Creighton adds that the craft was described as having a distinct rim around the edge, about three feet wide, and that it must have been the so-called Saturn or double washbowl type seen over Trinidad Island, in January, 1958 and photographed from a Brazilian navy vessel, one of the best authenticated photographs of UFOs.

Creighton also reports a contactee case from Argentina, involving a shopkeeper named Filipe Martinez, who claimed contact with UFOs on several occasions between 1949 and 1951 and again in 1965. While hunting in April, 1965, he saw a large craft hovering a few meters from the ground, about 300 meters away. It was egg-shaped and had some kind of rapidly revolving ring around it, and it was quiet. As he rushed toward it, he was struck by a kind of paralysis that stopped him in his tracks. A door opened in the craft and a small man descended to the ground on a narrow ladder. This man was no more than a meter in height and wore a helmet; there were two cables linking the helmet to the UFO. There was conversation, the stranger speaking slowly and apparently with difficulty. "He said that he and his people were friendly and that they came from near the moon." He referred to his UFO as being called a "sil" and promised to return for yet another meeting with Mr. Martinez.

Biologist Ivan Sanderson, in *Uninvited Visitors,* has this to say about the likelihood of UFOs originating within our solar system. "The likelihood of the material UAOs and UFOs coming from other planets in our solar system is of a fairly high order of probability. But whether they originated there and/or are indigenous to any such bodies is much less probable." (UAO, incidentally, stands for Unidentified Aerial Object.)

Despite the generally held beliefs that we know so much about our sister planets now that if there were any life on them we'd know it, Sanderson points out that "just because the moon and now Mars, are found to be pockmarked and therefore look dead, does not mean that they are—any more than our earth is. Don't forget the statements of our astronauts to the effect that *there is no indication of life down here from even a little way up*." In other words, when an alien pilot approaches earth, our planet looks just as dead as Mars and Venus look to us even from the comparative proximity of our space probes!

Perhaps one of the most puzzling cases recently brought to national prominence again in a televised documentary is the case of Lieutenant Colonel Robert Friend, USAF, former head of Project Blue Book, who is now in retirement. As reported by writer Robert Emenegger, Colonel

Friend followed up on a tip supplied to him by Rear Admiral K. concerning a trance medium in Maine who allegedly had contact with extraterrestrial beings. Two naval intelligence officers were sent to investigate the matter. In trance, the medium was able to answer scientific and very technical questions which she would not normally know or understand. Allegedly, she was able to do this with the help of extraterrestrials working through her.

"According to the report, she indicated there was an organization, OEEV, which meant Universal Association of Planets, and that organization had a project EU or EUENZA, meaning earth, which was being conducted." At this point the extraterrestrial entities informed the officers that they were willing to entrance one of the officers, a naval commander and intelligence officer who had never shown any indication of mediumship. The experiment was indeed successful. Colonel Friend entered the case then and satisfied himself that the naval commander in question was indeed able to go into trance and make contact with the supposed extraterrestrials. At one point Friend demanded to see a spaceship, whereupon the entranced commander informed Friend and his associates that he need only go to the window to have proof—and there it was, visible to all of them. The communicators claimed to be from the planet Uranus, from Jupiter, Mercury, and even a place called Centaurus. To this day, the incident has not been resolved. At the time his superiors told Colonel Friend to forget the whole thing, and so he did.

Until we land on these planets in our solar

system and investigate directly, we can't be entirely sure whether or not humanoids live on them. My earlier view was that nothing resembling humans existed in our solar system except on the third planet, earth, but I'm inclined to revise my earlier negative estimates to suggest that perhaps bases exist on some of these otherwise inhospitable planets, way stations between the outer reaches of space and us. That living beings totally different from us have adapted themselves to live without atmosphere or in atmospheres of several hundred degrees Fahrenheit and may exist on some of the planets of the solar system is ridiculous. Even if it were proved that some space travelers originate within our own solar system, chances are that the much larger portion of those coming here originate further out in space. They already know that the likelihood of life conditions similar to earth exist in millions of other locations. Compared to those far out places, conditions on the other planets of our solar system are not nearly as good.

We can be quite sure that humanoids come to us from Zeta Reticuli 1 and perhaps also from one of the other way stations visited by the Zeta Reticuli Ufonauts themselves, since they seem to indicate life-supporting planets. I respect Andrija Puharich and Uri Geller's testimonies concerning the Spectra, which Puharich describes as "a huge city that watches over a large chunk of this galaxy." In my interview with Dr. Puharich I wondered whether the inhabitants of Spectra, those satellite cities in the sky, were as mortal as we are or whether they were in any way different from us? Did they have physical bodies, for instance?

"Some do, like the people from Hoova whom I call Hovids; they say they live an average lifetime of one million earth years. They do have bodies but they cannot exist in our particular atmosphere since it is not compatible with them."

I asked Dr. Puharich whether he had ever had any indications that space people were kidnapping humans for experimental and other purposes. "Those are theories," he replied. "There are good guys and bad guys. I have never seen any of the bad guys myself, and I've been to the Bermuda Triangle, I've gone under the sea, I've interviewed people; things disappear but nobody can ever pin it down to a spaceship. I don't really subscribe to the John Keel view concerning little black men in Cadillacs. I don't see any of that spooky business. I mean, I've been out in the middle of nowhere in bush and in desert and in mountains, and I have seen spacecraft and I've had communication without any fear of being snatched or taken over. I think people overreact, and make big productions out of things. Especially when they are frightened."

"Why did your communicators insist on destroying your evidence, dematerializing the tapes?"

"They didn't want any hard evidence of their existence. They've always operated that way: if you look at the history of the last twenty-seven years of UFO sightings, you will find that nobody has gotten any hard evidence that they exist. I asked, 'Why are you so secretive?' They said, 'We're not secretive at all. We don't believe in revealing our intentions.' I said, 'You're all over the place. What are you trying to do?' They said, 'We're trying to get mankind used to our presence because eventually we are going to land on earth.' I replied, 'Why do you want to land?' They said, 'Well, mankind has been destroying itself anyway, and we think if man will accept our help that we can bail him out of this.' To which I replied, 'So why don't you land in Times Square, do the usual public relations stunt?' To that they replied, 'Well, look, we've got more experience than you. We've been handling the human race for thousands and thousands of years, and we know how they freak out, how they panic, how they abjectly worship us. We can't deal with them as equals. So we gradually have to let them get used to us.'"

I thought that over for a moment as we walked in Andrija's beautiful if somewhat wild garden at Ossining, New York. "Look," Puharich said, "I've got beautiful photographs of spaceships. Who cares? There are thousands of those and nobody believes them. They say they are faked."

"Do you know of any evidence that at least some of these aliens come from a specific place in our own galaxy?"

"The ones I have been dealing with do not come from our galaxy. They come from parts of the universe I don't think we even know about or understand. One of my patients, a girl up in Massachusetts who is totally blind and can see perfectly normally under hypnosis, even though she has no optic nerves, has contact with what she claims to be space people from a globular cluster outside of our galaxy called M-92. I can't prove it, I only have her statement."

Although Puharich's tapes have been destroyed, we do have some writings, samples which have survived the attempts of Ufonauts to leave no tangible evidence of their existence behind. In addition to the samples of writing, we have police officer Louis Zamora's sketch of the insignia he saw on the side of the UFO, an arrow within a frame arched in the upper half and rectangular in the lower half. Mr. Keel has obliged us by bringing together all the known writings and symbols observed on UFOs up to the present, in a section of his very useful book, *UFOs—Operation Trojan Horse*. He does not attempt to explain the strange symbols and writings, but it is extraordinary that witnesses from widely separate areas of earth, without any contact whatsoever with each other, should come up with similar or related symbols or specimens of writings. And last, but certainly not least, I have in my possession an entire manuscript of undeciphered writing, allegedly from space, received in trance by Alice McDermott Lombardo, waiting to be deciphered.

Charles Bowen, editor of the *Flying Saucer Review*, and *The Humanoids*, sums it up best, when he says, "What is going on? Did these witnesses, widely dispersed on earth, and in time, all have experiences with solid creatures from another world or from another dimension or reality?

Or did they all suffer hallucinations of a similar kind, where the dream creature seen was strikingly similar in many respects?" Mr. Bowen wonders whether some of the images represented by the incursions from space are not deliberate mock-ups, covering up for the real purpose behind the visits, whatever they may be.

There may be isolated instances of camouflage, of covering up the real intent of the expeditions in order not to upset humankind; but the real purpose of the aliens does not seem to be quite as complicated as some researchers may think. We represent an alien race to them, one that seems to be bent on self-destruction, living on a planet beset by natural catastrophes, disease, shortages, and all together not a well-ordered universe. Could it then be that they are simply exercising caution in their contacts with us, their lessers, not so much for our sake, but for their own? Are they perhaps protecting their far more advanced worlds from some sort of destructive fall-out from ours, or from contact with us? This is merely speculation. Until we can sit down with our space visitors and discuss this intelligently and without restrictions of any kind, we can't be sure of their reasons for what appears to be strange behavior. I don't think they are playing games with us; I think they are in earnest in their contacts, and I think that they do not consider us totally unworthy, otherwise why the attempts at mating with some of our healthier specimens, why the interest in crossbreeding of children? Obviously, we on earth have something they find attractive, and

I speak not only of metals heavier than iron.

UFO spaceship landings propelled by as yet unknown methods are not the product of hallucinations, but solid facts. Flesh and blood humanoids have come from these spaceships and related to certain individuals on earth. That much is fact. What, then, keeps them from making an orderly contact worthy of the superiority of their worlds? Perhaps it is the lack of an organization to which they could entrust such an arrangement, an organization that would represent not necessarily the governments of this world (always at odds with each other in political struggles for supremacy), but some non-political, scientifically oriented organization that would be dispassionate in its interest, yet interested in research to benefit humankind. At the same time, this group would not be so narrow-minded as to consider the "establishment" scientific level as the basis on which to build a bridge to UFO occupants.

Perhaps the various splinter groups now diligently researching UFO sightings and encounters might get together to elect a roof organization, dispatching into it their best talents, their leaders, to form an international body which would then be empowered to negotiate with the intelligences from space. I am convinced that only the existence of one such organization, well publicized, could induce the Ufonauts to make some sort of tangible, formal contact. Despite some disturbing indications that some humans might have been taken as specimens to worlds other than ours, and despite the somewhat impersonal approach to spot checks concerning the nature of humankind, as in the Barney and Betty Hill case, I think that our alien visitors are not bent on destroying us, but in their own way consider themselves the potential saviors of humankind from its own destructiveness.

## STAY IN TOUCH

On the following pages you will find listed, with their current prices, some of the books and tapes now available on related subjects. Your book dealer stocks most of these, and will stock new titles in the Llewellyn series as they become available. We urge your patronage.

To obtain a FREE COPY of our latest full CATALOG of New Age books, tapes, videos, crystals, products and services, just write to the address below. In each 80-page catalog sent out bimonthly, you will find articles, reviews, the latest information on New Age topics, a listing of news and events, and much more. It is an exciting and informative way to stay in touch with the New Age and the world. The first copy will be sent free of charge and you will continue receiving copies as long as you are an active customer. You may also subscribe to *The Llewellyn New Times* by sending a $2.00 donation ($7.00 for Canada & Mexico, and $20.00 for overseas). Order your copy of *The Llewellyn New Times* today!

*The Llewellyn New Times*
**P.O. Box 64383-Dept. 368, St. Paul, MN 55164**

## TO ORDER BOOKS AND PRODUCTS ON THE FOLLOWING PAGES:

If your book dealer does not carry the titles and products listed on the following pages, you may order them directly from Llewellyn. Please send full price in U.S. funds, plus $2.00 for postage and handling for the first book, and 50¢ for each additional book. There are no postage and handling charges for orders over $50. UPS Delivery: We ship UPS whenever possible. Delivery guaranteed. Provide your street address as UPS does not deliver to P.O. Boxes. UPS to Canada requires a $50 minimum order. Allow 4-6 weeks for delivery. Orders outside the U.S.A. and Canada: Airmail—add retail price of book; add $5 for each non-book item (tapes, etc.); add $1 per item for surface mail. You may use your major credit card to order these titles by calling 1-800-THE-MOON, M-F, 8:00-5:00, Central Time. Send orders to:

**LLEWELLYN PUBLICATIONS**
**P.O. Box 64383-Dept. 368**
**St.Paul, MN 55164, U.S.A.**

*Poltergeists ... Witchcraft ... UFOs ... Lost Civilizations ... Reincarnation ... Telepathy ... Channelers ... Crystals ... Out-of-Body Travel ... Psychic Healing ... Weird Creatures ...*

## Each and Every Month, Leave Your World ... and Enter the Unknown Realms of FATE

For more than 40 years, FATE has existed to give you what no one else does: the latest-breaking events, evidence and discoveries in the world of the paranormal. FATE *won't* give you rehashes of the same old reports you've heard for years. Get the most bold and exciting exploration of the strange and mysterious available in this galaxy! To receive your one-year (12-month) subscription, see the instructions below. Don't miss another spellbinding month ... Order Now.

### SUBSCRIBE TODAY! HERE'S HOW

✓ SAVE 37% off the cover price of $23.40. You save $8.45!

✓ SATISFACTION 100% GUARANTEED. If you are not delighted at any time, you may cancel and receive a full refund on all unmailed issues.

✓ Send your name, address, city, state and zip code along with a check or money order for $14.95 to FATE Magazine, P.O. Box 1940, 170 Future Way, Marion, OH 43305.

## THE GOBLIN UNIVERSE
### by Ted Holiday and Colin Wilson

Throughout history, we have been confronted with things that fail to fit squarely into our self-conceived reality. Many times we find them frightening. Even modern science is fearful and rejects those things for which it presently does not have any explanation—things such as UFOs and the many things that go bump in the night.

It is the world of the mind that is the Goblin Universe—goblin only because of our own limitations. And it is this greater universe that is the place of magick, of psychic phenomena, of ghosts and poltergeists, UFOs and the Men in Black, dragons and yetis and the Loch Ness Monster, of prophecy and retrogression and other mysteries.

Ted Holiday and Colin Wilson explore this amazing world with accounts of Ted Holiday's personal experiences and his search for a "unified theory" to open our perceptions to the full universe. Wilson sees the problem in terms of the built-in nature of the human brain and our lack of training in its use.

Holiday and Wilson examine a wide range of "occult" phenomena and explore the technologies by which we may expand our world. Wilson speculates, for example, that some people are able to unconsciously (and can learn to do so consciously) tap actual "earth energies" with the right brain and direct them to bring about change and movement in the physical world—as in the case of poltergeist and psychokinetic phenomena.

**0-87542-310-8, 288 pgs., 5 1/4 x 8, photos       $9.95**

## EXTRA-TERRESTRIALS AMONG US
### by George Andrews

According to a law already on the books, which may be activated whenever the government wishes to enforce it, anyone found guilty of E.T. contact is to be quarantined indefinitely under armed guard. Does that sound like the government doesn't take Extra-Terrestrials seriously? This book blows the lid off the government's cover-up about UFOs and their occupants, setting the stage for a "Cosmic Watergate."

Author George Andrews researched the evidence concerning extra-terrestrial intervention in human affairs for over a decade before presenting his startling conclusions. *Extra-Terrestrials Among Us* is an exciting challenge to "orthodox" thinking, and will certainly broaden the reader's perception of the world we live in.

You are given direct information as to *why* E.T.s are here, case history descriptions of their varying appearances, and what they are trying to accomplish. You will also learn how to determine whether an alien contact is beneficial or harmful. *Most* E.T.s come to rejuvenate the Earth and aid in the evolutionary development of humankind. Human contacts are the vanguard of an experiment that will be expanded in our near future.

**0-87542-010-9, 300 pgs., 5 1/4 x 8, photos**                                    **$9.95**

## A PRACTICAL GUIDE TO PAST LIFE REGRESSION
### by Florence Wagner McClain

Have you ever felt that there had to be more to life than this? Have you ever met someone and felt an immediate kinship? Have you ever visited a strange place and felt that you had been there before? Have you struggled with frustrations and fears which seem to have no basis in your present life? Are you afraid of death? Have you ever been curious about reincarnation or maybe just interested enough to be skeptical?

This book presents a simple technique which you can use to obtain past life information TODAY. There are no mysterious preparations, no groups to join, no philosophy to which you must adhere. You don't even have to believe in reincarnation. The tools are provided for you to carry out your own investigations, find your own answers and make your own judgments as to the validity of the information and its usefulness to you.

Whether or not you believe in reincarnation, past life regression remains a powerful and valid tool for self-exploration. Information procured through this procedure can be invaluable for personal growth and inner healing, no matter what its source. Florence McClain's guidebook is an eminently sane and capable guide for those who wish to explore their possible past lives or conduct regressions themselves.

0-87542-510-0, 160 pgs., 5 1/4 x 8, softcover          $6.95

## THE LLEWELLYN PRACTICAL GUIDE
## TO THE DEVELOPMENT OF PSYCHIC POWERS
## by Denning & Phillips

You may not realize it, but you already have the ability to exercise and develop ESP, astral vision, clairvoyance, divination, dowsing, prophecy, and communication with spirits.

Written by two of the most knowledgeable experts in the world of Magick today, this book is a complete course—teaching you, step-by-step, how to develop these powers that actually have been yours since birth. Using the techniques they teach, you will soon be able to move objects at a distance, see into the future, know the thoughts and feelings of others, find lost objects, locate water and even people using your own no-longer latent talents.

Psychic powers are as much a natural ability as any other talent. You'll learn to play with these new skills, work with groups of friends to accomplish things you never would have believed possible before reading this book. The text shows you how to make the equipment you can use, the exercises you can do—many of them anytime, anywhere—and how to use your abilities to change your life and the lives of those close to you. Many of the exercises are presented in forms that can be adapted as games for pleasure and fun, as well as development.

**0-87542-191-1, 256 pgs., 5 1/4 x 8, illus., softcover         $7.95**